Heidi Doxey

TIME TO SHARE

52 Weeks of Primary Planning

CFI
An Imprint of Cedar Fort, Inc.
Springville, Utah

ISBN 13: 978-1-4621-1703-1

Published by CFI, an imprint of Cedar Fort, Inc.
2373 W. 700 S., Springville, UT 84663
Distributed by Cedar Fort, Inc., www.cedarfort.com

LIBRARY OF CONGRESS CONTROL NUMBER: 2015951868

Cover design by Shawnda T. Craig
Cover design © 2015 Lyle Mortimer
Edited and typeset by Kevin Haws

Printed in the United States of America

10 9 8 7 6 5 4 3 2 1

Printed on acid-free paper

Dedicated to the Springville 9th Ward Primary
(past and present), especially Abby, Brylie, Chrisara, Claire,
Dessie, Ellie, Gloria, Lexi, Lkayla, and Jo Jo.

Contents

Contents

Introduction

The scriptures can help us build our relationship with Heavenly Father, our personal testimonies, and our ability to seek out and find revelation for ourselves and those we love.

They are powerful tools in our lives. When we make scripture study a habit and "search the scriptures diligently," we will "wax strong in the knowledge of truth" (Alma 17:2), just as the sons of Mosiah did. The truths and strength we find in the scriptures will help us battle Satan and build up the kingdom of God.

Our children need this strength to resist the temptations of our time. They need to know that God's word is still applicable to them, and we need to teach them how to find those treasures in the scriptures for themselves.

I hope that as we all become better acquainted with the scriptures throughout this year, we will each discover new insights, personal revelation, and more ways to relate scripture stories and lessons to our own lives. I know that the scriptures are true, and I am so grateful to have God's word available to me every day.

HOW TO USE THIS BOOK

This book is designed to help you prepare for Primary with ideas for sharing time, talks, scriptures, singing, and more. For each chapter, you will find an overview of several resources that can be used throughout the month. Next you will find specific ideas for each week in the month, including talks and scriptures your Primary children can give. Each week also includes a reverence idea and a sharing time activity or lesson. With a little adaptation, these lessons and activities can also be used in your home for family night or family scripture study.

The last two chapters of the book focus on ideas and tips for singing time and the annual Primary presentation, with suggestions for parents, teachers, and leaders.

MONTHLY OVERVIEW

Multimedia Resources

In recent years, the Church has created a wonderful library of videos and other materials that can be accessed online. For each month, you'll find a suggested list of multimedia resources (with links) that you can find online and use at any point throughout the month. Some children learn best by having materials presented to them visually, so these resources can be a great way to engage those who might otherwise have a hard time paying attention. Before using one of these resources in Primary, be sure to download the material to your device or check to make sure that you can stream it quickly at church.

Songs

The songs listed at the beginning of the month will help you prepare for your annual Primary program. Anytime you see a bolded song title, that is one of the songs that is specifically meant to be included in your annual Primary program. By focusing on one or two of these songs each month, you won't have to learn all-new material just before you give the program. In addition to these songs, you'll also find some more songs listed that fit in with the theme for that month, as well as a few classic favorites that can be used all year long. More ideas and tips for singing time are included in the second-to last-chapter of the book. Note: Unless otherwise specified, all songs are from the *Children's Songbook*.

Gospel Art Book

Each month also includes a suggested picture from the *Gospel Art Book* that can be displayed on your Primary board or at the front of the room. You can refer to this picture throughout the month as a visual reminder to the children of that month's specific theme. Changing the picture monthly will help to keep it fresh in their minds.

WEEKLY SECTIONS

Attention Activity

The attention activity at the beginning of each weekly section is meant to help your children prepare for Primary and get ready to feel the Spirit. It can be done as children are arriving while you are preparing for opening exercises. You need not wait until every child is seated before beginning these activities.

These activities are not meant to take up a lot of time—only a minute or two. They will help you grab your children's attention and get them ready to reverently participate in Primary. Of course, with younger children especially, you can't expect silence to last, so you may choose to save this attention activity until just before your lesson or even mid-lesson rather than doing it at the beginning.

Scripture

A weekly scripture reference will help you find scriptures for a child to give as part of your opening exercises. You may also want to encourage children to share an article of faith in addition to the scripture for the week.

Talk

Each week includes a sample talk or story, in addition to the lesson, that would be appropriate for a child to give in Primary. These talks can also be used during the lesson or in family home evening or another setting. While the stories and language are simple, the concepts and doctrine may not be. To foster understanding, you may want to have the child giving the talk illustrate a few of the main ideas or share how this story relates to his or her own life. At the end of the talk, have the child bear a brief testimony.

Lesson

The lessons included with each week are meant to help leaders, teachers, and parents prepare for sharing time, a class lesson, or family home evening. The basic structure of the lessons is to begin with a discussion, followed by an activity, an application section, and then a brief review. You may wish to use only part of the lesson or modify it

Introduction

to fit the needs of your children. The Spirit will help you to know how best to teach the principles you want to convey.

The lessons have been designed to involve minimal preparation and planning. While they may include some movement or active participation by children, they are also meant to be reverent enough to be done in a church building on Sunday. At times, you may need to remind the children that they are in a house of the Lord and that their voices, behavior, and tone should always reflect that. Of course, it's also important to enjoy learning together. Use your best judgment about whether these activities will work for your children.

With a little adaptation, these lessons and activities can be used by a large or small Primary, class, or family. For example, instead of picking one or two children to volunteer, you may want to let every child have a turn. You will need the Spirit's guidance to help you adapt your planning to fit the children you serve. Remember that each one is a child of God and each one wants to be included. If you have children with special needs or circumstances, do your best to be sensitive to them, even if it means changing your original plan.

Please note that this book is not meant to supersede or take precedence in any way over the Church's curriculum. It simply contains some additional ideas for busy teachers and parents. Whether you use it in your home, at church, or for another activity, I hope it will be a helpful resource to you so that you can spend your time focusing on the children you love and the eternal principles you want to them to learn.

Chapter 1: January
God Speaks to Us through the Scriptures

MULTIMEDIA RESOURCES

"Daily Bread: Pattern"—YouTube, Mormon Channel, 2:52

"A Book of Mormon Story"—YouTube, Mormon Channel, 5:16

"Scriptures Legacy"—Mormon Channel, 22:30

"Reflecting God's Love—What Scriptures Mean to Me"—Mormon Channel, 3:27

"If I Listen with My Heart"—General conference, 4:26 (https://www.youtube.com/watch?v=_z8L0nPA3Ew)

SONG LIST

Focus Song: "If I Listen with My Heart"—*Friend*, January 2011, available online http://www.defordmusic.com/sheet-music/alphabetical-list/if-i-listen-with-my-heart/

Additional Songs: "Search, Ponder, and Pray" (109), "Seek the Lord Early" (108)

GOSPEL ART BOOK

"Joseph Smith Seeks Wisdom in the Bible" (89)

Week 1: The Scriptures Contain the Word of God

ATTENTION ACTIVITY

Invite two children to stand at the front of the room and read 2 Nephi 32:3, trading off reading first by five words at a time, then three, two, and finally trading off every other word. For junior Primary, have one child stand up with a teacher. For a child who cannot yet read, have the teacher whisper the words for the child to say out loud.

SCRIPTURE

Articles of Faith 1:8

TALK

Nephi and his family knew that they had to go on a big trip—one that would take them across the ocean to a new land. They packed many things to take with them, but they forgot to pack something very important—their scriptures. Heavenly Father told them to return to Jerusalem to get the scriptures. These scriptures were written on gold plates.

The man who owned the gold plates was named Laban. He did not want to give the plates to Nephi's family. But Heavenly Father prepared a way. He told Nephi to keep trying, and when nothing else worked, Heavenly Father told Nephi to kill Laban.

Nephi did not want to kill Laban, but he obeyed. Nephi knew that it would be better for Laban to die than for all of Nephi's family to forget about Heavenly Father. Nephi also knew that the scriptures help us to remember Heavenly Father because Heavenly Father speaks to us and teaches us through the scriptures.

LESSON

Discussion: Show the children a phone, tablet, and laptop, or just photos of these things. Explain how these devices help us get information.

- How else do we receive information?
- How do we receive information from Heavenly Father? (The scriptures)

Tell the children that we have four standard works. Together, they present the fulness of the gospel. We also consider the words of our modern prophets and Apostles to be like scriptures for our day. Discuss what is contained in each of the four standard works.

ACTIVITY

Read the following descriptions of people from the scriptures. Have the children raise their hands as soon as they can guess who the person is and which of the four standard works tells of his or her life.

My name is _____. I was born long before Jesus was born. The people in my city wanted to build a tower to get to heaven, but this was not right. Heavenly Father guided my brother to lead our family and friends to a new land. We traveled in barges across the ocean and came to a land of promise. (Jared, Book of Mormon)

My name is _____. For a long time, I wanted to have children. I prayed that Heavenly Father would bless me with a son. I promised Heavenly Father that I would teach my son to be righteous and serve the Lord his whole life. (Hannah, Old Testament)

My name is _____. When I was young, I lived in a land called Ur. Many people there worshipped idols and false gods. They tried to sacrifice me on an altar as part of their idol worship, but the Lord saved me. (Abraham, Pearl of Great Price or Old Testament)

My name is _____. When I was a teenager, my brother had a vision from Heavenly Father. He learned that God's Church was no longer on the earth. My brother restored the gospel in the latter days. We were good friends. We worked together to build the kingdom, and when my brother was arrested, so was I. We were killed by an angry mob. (Hyrum Smith, Doctrine and Covenants)

APPLICATION

Ask younger children to fill in the blank in the following statement: The scriptures tell me to _____.

If time permits, have them color a picture of something the scriptures tell them to do.

Have older children share their favorite verse of scripture or their favorite story from the scriptures. Ask them why they like it and what it means to them.

Time to Share

REVIEW

Tell the children how blessed we are to have the scriptures available to us all the time through modern technology. If you brought your phone, tablet, or laptop, show them the Gospel Library app or the Church's website. You may also want to play an audio clip from the scriptures. Encourage the children to study the scriptures and interact with them in a way that's best for them and helps them feel the Spirit. Bear your testimony of the importance of scripture study.

Week 2: I Need to Study the Scriptures Often

ATTENTION ACTIVITY

Ask a volunteer to come to the front of the room to act like one of the following animals. If they want to make sounds, have them do so quietly. Invite the other children to guess what animal the volunteer is. Then choose another volunteer for the next animal. Depending on how long it takes the children to guess, you may only have time for two or three animals.

- a hen pecking for seeds
- a cow chewing cud
- a horse eating an apple
- a giraffe reaching up for leaves to eat
- a monkey peeling a banana
- a bear catching a fish

SCRIPTURE

2 Nephi 32:3

TALK

Lincoln wants to learn to play the piano. His parents help him find a teacher, who tells him that he will need to practice. At first, Lincoln is excited. On the day after his lesson, he practices for more than an hour. But the next day, he's too busy playing football to practice piano. After a few more days, Lincoln decides to practice again, but he soon gets distracted by something his sister is watching. And then it's time to eat dinner.

The next week, when Lincoln is getting ready for his piano lesson, he has hardly practiced at all. Even though he wants to learn how to play the piano, he needs to turn practicing into a habit. His teacher reminds him that the only way to get better is to practice often.

One habit we all need is to study the scriptures—every day, if we can. When we study the scriptures, we are feeding our spirit bodies. Just like our physical bodies, our spirits need food every day. And when we read the scriptures, our spirits can grow big and strong!

Time to Share

LESSON

Discussion: If you have not already done so, read 2 Nephi 32:3. Ask the children what it means to feast on the words of Christ.

- How is feasting different from pecking like a hen or chewing like a cow? (See attention activity above.)
- Why are we counseled to make scripture study a daily habit?

ACTIVITY

Teach the children how to fight Satan's lies with the scriptures. Explain that Satan often tries to tempt us by telling us lies, but the scriptures teach us the truth. Assign each class a scripture from the following list. Have them read it with their teacher. Once they are done, read aloud one of the false teachings below and ask the children to raise their hands if they think their class's scripture can fight the lie. Identify the class with the correct scripture and have a child in that class explain how the scripture relates to the false teaching. Keep reading the statements until you have matched them all with their corresponding scriptures.

Scripture Reference	False Teaching
Joseph Smith—History 1:25	God doesn't speak to us today.
2 Nephi 28:8–11	We can do whatever we want and Heavenly Father won't punish us too much.
1 Corinthians 15:19–20, 22	There is no such thing as life after death.
Ether 3:14	Jesus was just a regular person.
Galatians 2:16	If we do enough good, we can earn a place in heaven all by ourselves.

APPLICATION

Help each child set a scripture study goal for the year. Have the children write it on two slips of paper: one for them to keep and one to keep at church. Throughout the year, when children complete their goals, invite them to share their experience with the rest of the Primary. Then display the slip of paper for the completed goal somewhere in your Primary room.

Some examples of goals:
- Listen to the entire Book of Mormon.
- Memorize a specific passage or a certain number of verses.
- Read all four gospels in the New Testament.
- Write a talk on a gospel topic using five scripture references.

REVIEW

Share your own method for studying the scriptures and tell about a time when your scripture study helped you to choose the right or inspired you with personal revelation about a specific question. Bear witness that the scriptures can help our spirits grow and give us power to resist temptation.

Week 3: I Am Blessed for Obeying the Words of God in the Scriptures

ATTENTION ACTIVITY

Show the video "Book of Mormon Stories (6/54): Lehi's Dream"—Mormon Channel, 11/15/11 (https://www.youtube.com/watch?v=n3KbdQzxNDQ).

SCRIPTURE

D&C 35:20

TALK

Many people knew about Jesus before He was born. They looked forward to His birth, life, Atonement, and Resurrection. Some of them wrote down what they learned about Jesus. These writings were prophecies because they talked about things that had not happened yet. Over time, the prophecies became scriptures.

Later, when Jesus was born, the prophecies were fulfilled, and this helped the people in Jesus's day to know that He really was the Savior. But in order to know for sure, the people needed to know what was in the prophecies—they needed to read their scriptures.

The Wise Men who came to worship Jesus after He was born had read their scriptures. They knew exactly where to look for Jesus. They knew they needed to follow the new star that had appeared. Because they read their scriptures, the Wise Men knew how to find Jesus. When we read the scriptures today, they tell us how to find Jesus and return to live with Him someday.

LESSON

Discussion: If you have an instruction manual for a car, bring it with you to Primary. Show it to the children, including any charts or diagrams inside. Explain that this manual teaches you how to use the car. If you do not have a car manual, bring another type of manual, or describe what a manual is like. Then ask these questions:

- How are the scriptures like an instruction manual? What instructions do they give us?
- If we follow the instructions in the scriptures, what will they help us to do?

ACTIVITY

Draw a long line on a chalkboard or a large piece of paper. At one end of the line, draw a tree. At the other end, place a magnet or a piece of masking tape. Tell the children that the magnet or tape represents Lehi and his family. The line is the iron rod. Lehi needs to follow the iron rod to get to the tree, where he will be happy.

Read the following actions, and for each one ask the children if this would move Lehi and his family closer or farther from the iron rod and the tree. Then move the magnet or piece of tape accordingly. After you finish reading the statements below, if Lehi has not yet reached the tree, ask the children what else he could do to move forward.

- obeying the Word of Wisdom
- making fun of someone
- having family scripture study
- singing Church songs
- telling a lie
- making a card for someone who is sick
- praying for the missionaries
- getting angry and yelling at someone
- cheating in a game
- doing chores
- inviting a friend to a Church activity
- saying sorry
- smiling at someone new

APPLICATION

Explain that each of the actions that brought Lehi closer to the tree is discussed in the scriptures. Ask the children to think of something they could do to draw nearer to Heavenly Father. Then call on someone to give an answer. For each good answer given, find a scripture that mentions this idea. Show older children how to find a scripture to match their idea by using the Topical Guide or searching on the Gospel Library app. For younger children, try to think of a scripture story that matches their idea.

Time to Share

Child's Answer	Scripture Story
We should pray	Enos, Daniel, Joseph Smith
We should read the scriptures	Josiah, Ezra, Mormon, John Taylor
We should be kind	Jesus, the Good Samaritan, Naomi and Ruth

REVIEW

Remind the children that Heavenly Father speaks to us through the scriptures. He prepared these sacred books for our day, and He wants us to do what the scriptures tell us to do. When we do, He will bless us. Share a brief testimony of a time when you felt blessed for obeying the words of God in the scriptures.

Week 4: I Can Have a Testimony of the Scriptures

ATTENTION ACTIVITY

Play the telephone game. Whisper a short sentence to one child and have the child repeat it to the next person, then so on until the message reaches the last person. Compare the message at the end to what it was at the beginning. If you have a large Primary, divide into groups of six to ten so that everyone can participate.

SCRIPTURE

Alma 5:46

TALK

Leona loves to visit her family's cabin in the mountains. There is so much to see and do at the cabin. She loves to smell the fresh mountain air, look for colorful wildflowers, and eat the yummy hamburgers her dad likes to barbecue there. Leona also loves the feel of the soft warm blankets on the bed in the cabin and the sound of the cool breeze blowing through the trees at night. When Leona is at the cabin, she can learn a lot about the world around her by using her senses. She can smell, see, taste, feel, and hear new things. And those things are part of what make the cabin special for her.

But Leona can also feel with her spirit at the cabin. She can feel love for Heavenly Father and His beautiful creations and feel the love of her family as they go hiking and play games together. When Leona is at the cabin, it's easy for her to remember that Heavenly Father loves her because she can feel that immense love with her spirit every time she visits.

LESSON

Discussion: Ask the children what their favorite foods are. Then ask what their favorite sights and smells are. Explain that we use our bodies to experience and learn about the physical world around us. But each of us also has a spirit that can learn. Our spirits do not learn things in the same way that our bodies do, but the things we learn by the spirit are still true, even if we cannot see or touch them.

Time to Share

- How do we learn by the spirit?
- When we read the scriptures, do we learn with our bodies or with our spirits?

Explain that everyone feels the Spirit differently, but we can know that we are feeling the Spirit if we feel happy, if our minds seem clearer, or if the things we are feeling make us want to do good.

ACTIVITY

On the board, write, "I know the scriptures are true because . . ." and give the children pieces of paper and crayons and help them copy the sentence onto their papers. Then have the children complete the sentence with their personal testimonies of the scriptures in the form of a sentence or short paragraph. If they are too young to write, ask them to draw a picture to finish the sentence. Have them keep their papers.

APPLICATION

Read this quote from Boyd K. Packer: "A testimony is to be found in the bearing of it! . . . To speak out is the test of your faith" (*Ensign*, January 1983, 54). Encourage the children to share their testimonies by giving their pieces of paper to a family member, a friend, or someone else. They may also want to give the person a copy of the Book of Mormon. Tell them that just as the Spirit has helped them to learn that the scriptures are true, the Spirit can also help them choose someone to bear their testimony to.

REVIEW

Share a brief story of a time when you learned something by the Spirit and not with your body. Help the children understand that as we grow and progress, we do not always feel the Spirit in the same way we did when we were young. Sometimes it may seem that Heavenly Father is far away, but we can draw nearer to Him as we read the scriptures.

Chapter 2: February
I Can Learn about Heavenly Father's Plan in the Scriptures

MULTIMEDIA RESOURCES

"Our Eternal Life—What Do Mormons Believe?"—YouTube, Mormon Channel, 3:46 (https://www.youtube.com/watch?v=9MiF_HKoFr4)

"We Lived with God"—YouTube, Mormon Channel, 4:00 (https://www.youtube.com/watch?v=JR8qIrJcJh4)

"Jesus Is Resurrected"—YouTube, Mormon Channel, 4:05 (https://www.youtube.com/watch?v=MlKetn7ZiNU)

"Families Can Be Together Forever"—YouTube, Mormon Channel, 3:10 (https://www.youtube.com/watch?v=0J-_f4oRuWI)

"I Am a Child of God"—YouTube, Mormon Channel, 2:55 (https://www.youtube.com/watch?v=JOrcqqpHCt8)

SONG LIST

Focus Song: "I Will Follow God's Plan" (164–65)

Additional Songs: "Families Can Be Together Forever" (188), "I Lived in Heaven" (4), "I Am a Child of God" (2)

Review Song: "If I Listen with My Heart"

GOSPEL ART BOOK

"The Lord Created All Things" (2)

Week 1: Heavenly Father Has a Plan for Our Happiness

ATTENTION ACTIVITY

Display a photo of a baby. On the board, put blank spaces to fill in the letters of the words *premortal life*. Ask the children if they know where the baby lived before being born. Have them guess letters or come up to the board to write in one letter per person until all the letters are filled in.

SCRIPTURE

2 Nephi 9:13

TALK

Joseph Smith learned many things during his time as prophet. One of the most exciting happened when he learned about Heavenly Father's plan of salvation. Joseph's older brother Alvin died when Joseph was only a teenager. Joseph loved his brother Alvin. The Smith family was very sad when Alvin died.

Years later, Joseph had a vision. He saw Alvin in the celestial kingdom. Joseph knew then that he would see his brother again someday. Through Heavenly Father's plan, each of us can live with our families forever.

Heavenly Father wants us to return and live with Him. His plan will help us become like Him. The scriptures teach us about Heavenly Father's plan. When we follow the plan, we can be happy forever.

LESSON

Discussion and Activity: Tell the children that you are going to have them do a few things to symbolize Heavenly Father's plan. Remind them that before we lived on earth, we lived in heaven. Then we were born. Invite the children to stand up (symbolizing birth). We came to earth to gain bodies, have experiences, and prepare to return to Heavenly Father. Invite the children to reverently walk around the room to symbolize our earth life as you play the song "My Heavenly Father Loves Me" (228). At the end of the song, have the children sit down in their seats again. Tell them that sitting down symbolizes death. Everyone will die, but Heavenly Father has made it possible for us to live again. Jesus came to earth to set an example. He died and was resurrected so that each of us can be resurrected also.

- What does it mean to atone?
- Why was Jesus the only one who could die for us?

After your discussion, invite the children to stand up again. Tell them that this symbolizes the resurrection, when we will all receive glorious, perfect bodies. Those who are righteous will receive celestial bodies and live with Heavenly Father forever.

APPLICATION

Ask the children how knowing that Heavenly Father has a plan for us changes the way we live here on earth. Read Alma 34:32. Explain that right now is a time for us to choose the right, learn to repent, and prepare for eternity. Encourage the children to think of something they could do this week to follow Heavenly Father's plan. Examples:

- Give service to a family member.
- Repent for a wrong choice and try to do better.
- Help with family history work.
- Be kind to someone at school.

REVIEW

Help the children to understand that our lives on earth are not the beginning or the end of our existence. Share with them your testimony of the plan of salvation and why it matters to you and your family. Tell them what it means to have an eternal perspective and encourage them to keep that perspective. No matter what happens in their lives, they can always know that God has a plan for them.

Week 2: Jesus Created the World

ATTENTION ACTIVITY

Bring a small container of building blocks, Legos, or another kind of construction toy. Invite two or three children to come to the front of the room and create something while the other children watch. Give them a minute or two. When they are done, have them share what they made and leave their creations on display.

SCRIPTURE

Moses 2:27, 31

TALK

One time, a wicked man named Korihor tried to convince people that there was no Christ. He told them they could do whatever they wanted to do to be happy, and they didn't need to worry about sinning or repenting.

Alma knew Korihor was wrong. The people brought Korihor to see Alma. Korihor told Alma that if God would show them a sign, Korihor would believe in Jesus. But Alma told him that he didn't need a sign because "all things [tell us] there is a God" (Alma 30:44).

If Korihor had paid attention, he would have seen the beautiful world around him. Our world tells us that there is a God because God and Jesus Christ created it. They worked together to make the earth for us. They wanted us to come to earth to grow and learn to be good.

LESSON

Discussion: If you used the attention activity, point out the children's creations. Discuss how the children had no plan for what they were creating. Explain that when Heavenly Father and Jesus created the earth, they made a plan for it first. Everything was created spiritually before it was created physically. When everything was ready, Jesus created the earth.

- Why is it important to have a plan when you want to create something beautiful?

Jesus and Heavenly Father also created Adam and Eve to live on the earth. Adam and Eve taught their children how to work hard and obey Heavenly Father. Together, they created the first family on earth.

ACTIVITY

Play a matching game to help you remember the different periods of the Creation. On sheets of paper, write the numbers one through seven. Then on more papers, draw simple illustrations of the following creations. (If you have time during Primary, you could have each class illustrate one or two, or simply print out photos and bring them from home.)

1. Light and darkness
2. Water
3. Land and plants
4. Sun, moon, and stars
5. Fish, sea animals, and birds
6. Mammals and insects
7. Adam and Eve

Mix up the papers and then tape them all to the board, face down. Have the children take turns guessing two papers at a time to try and find a match.

APPLICATION

Because we are children of a Creator, each one of us has special talents that help us create and appreciate beauty in the world. Encourage the children to take time this week to enjoy Heavenly Father's creations. Remind them to thank Heavenly Father for the earth He made for us. Tell them how important it is for us to take good care of the earth. You may want to allow time for older children to write a list of creations they are most thankful for. With younger children, you could ask them to raise their hands and share their favorite creations.

REVIEW

Express gratitude for the world we live in. Share with the children some of your favorite places to visit in nature. You may want to show them pictures. Encourage them to spend time outdoors (weather permitting) and notice how complex and beautiful nature can be. Testify that God loves each of His creations, especially His children.

Week 3: Heavenly Father Gave Us Families

ATTENTION ACTIVITY

Watch "Musical Presentation: The Family Is of God"—YouTube, Church general conference, 5:14 (https://www.youtube.com/watch?v=GIyHi_bMTxE).

SCRIPTURE

"Happiness in family life is most likely to be achieved when founded upon the teachings of the Lord Jesus Christ. Successful marriages and families are established and maintained on principles of faith, prayer, repentance, forgiveness, respect, love, compassion, work, and wholesome recreational activities" ("The Family: A Proclamation to the World," paragraph 7).

TALK

Sarah, Nate, Brenna, and Aubrey love going on vacations with their family. They especially love getting together with their grandparents aunts, uncles, and cousins. They play games, tell stories, and eat ice cream. Sarah loves her big family.

Sarah's best friend, Addie, doesn't have a big family. Addie lives with her mom and dad. She doesn't have any brothers, sisters, aunts, uncles, or cousins. But she still loves her little family. They have lots of fun together and try to love and serve each other every day.

God has given each of us a family. Some families are big; some are small. Some are related by blood; others are related by love. It doesn't matter what size your family is or who is in it. The important thing is to be kind to each other, work together, and choose the right. When you do those things, you can live happily with your family forever. That's why Heavenly Father's plan is called the plan of happiness.

LESSON

Discussion: Remind the children that we lived with Heavenly Father before we were born. When He presented His plan to us, He told us that we would come to earth and be part of a family. Ask the following:

- Why do you think you were sent to your family?
- What makes your family special?

- How can you show the members of your family that you love each one of them?

Explain that Heavenly Father wanted us to come to earth to learn to love like He does. Our families are designed to teach us how to love and serve one another.

ACTIVITY

Prepare slips of paper before the lesson with the following roles written or printed on them.

- Love and care for husband.
- Love and care for wife.
- Love and care for children.
- Rear children in love and righteousness.
- Provide for the physical and spiritual needs of children.
- Teach children to love and serve one another.
- Teach children to observe the commandments of God.
- Teach children to be law-abiding citizens wherever they live.
- Honor marital vows with complete fidelity.
- Preside over their families in love and righteousness.
- Provide the necessities of life and protection for their families.
- Nurture children.
- Help one another as equal partners.
- Have faith.
- Pray together.
- Repent.
- Forgive one another.
- Show respect.
- Love each other.
- Be compassionate.
- Work together.
- Enjoy wholesome recreational activities.

Write the words *father*, *mother*, *parents*, and *family* on the board. Place the papers in a bag or bowl. Invite one child at a time to come up and choose a piece of paper. Have the child identify whose role it is and tape the piece of paper underneath the correct word. Refer to the family proclamation if you are not sure.

Time to Share

APPLICATION

Show the children a small heart cut out of paper. Explain that when we show love for the people in our family, we help our family become stronger. Ask them to think of one way they could strengthen their families this week through serving or showing love for a family member. Pass the heart to the first child and ask what he or she plans to do. Then have the first child pass the heart to the next person and so on until everyone has had a chance to share his or her plan.

REVIEW

Share with the children how important it is to be committed to families as the fundamental unit of society. Though times may change, families will always be central to our Heavenly Father's plan. Add your own thoughts on the blessings that come from being part of a family.

Week 4: I Want to Follow Heavenly Father's Plan

ATTENTION ACTIVITY

Invite two children to the front of the room. Have one child slowly walk backward from one end of the room to the other without looking forward. Have the other child act as a guide. Then have the children switch places or ask for another two children to volunteer.

SCRIPTURE

Proverbs 3:5–6

TALK

All day long, Nova makes choices. She gets to choose what to eat for breakfast, what to wear, and whether or not she's going to make her bed. Some of her choices are between right and wrong, like when she chooses to share her toys at the park instead of being greedy and keeping them for herself. Some of her choices are between two good things, like whether to read a book about dinosaurs or dancing princesses at bedtime.

Most of the time, Nova chooses the right. But when she makes a wrong choice, she knows she needs to say sorry and repent.

Learning to make good choices is important because every time we choose the right, we are following Heavenly Father's plan. He wants us to become like Him and return to live with Him someday. We can only do that if we choose to follow His plan by making good decisions.

LESSON

Discussion: Remind the children of the attention activity (if you used it) and explain that this is how time works on earth. We never know what is coming ahead of us. All we can do is look backward at what has passed. But our Heavenly Father knows the end from the beginning. He guides us through personal revelation because He knows what will be best for us. His plans for us are wonderful.

Tell the children that Heavenly Father's plan of happiness is meant for all of His children, but He also has individual plans for each one of us. We each have important callings to fulfill in life and talents to share.

Time to Share ·

- Why is it important to seek personal revelation when we make decisions?
- How does Heavenly Father guide us to the people He wants us to serve and the places He wants us to be?

Emphasize that no matter what plans Heavenly Father has for us, we need to do our part by choosing the right.

ACTIVITY

Read the following story. Instruct the children to listen carefully for the words *chose* and *choice*. Anytime you read one of those words, pause at the end of the sentence and have the children stand up if the choice was good or sit down if it was bad.

Ammon was a Nephite prince. His father, Mosiah, was a righteous king, but when Ammon was young, he and his brothers CHOSE to make fun of people who believed in Jesus. Then one day, an angel came to tell them to repent. Ammon CHOSE to listen to the angel and repent.

Later Ammon and his brothers CHOSE to become missionaries to the Lamanites. Mosiah knew that Ammon's CHOICE was good, but Mosiah was worried about his sons. Mosiah CHOSE to pray. The Lord told Mosiah that his sons would be protected while they were missionaries.

So Ammon and his brothers traveled to the Lamanite lands. They split up, and soon Ammon was found by a group of Lamanites. The Lamanites CHOSE to arrest Ammon and take him to their king. King Lamoni asked Ammon why he was there. Ammon CHOSE to tell the king that he wanted to live with the Lamanites and serve them. Lamoni was pleased with Ammon. He asked Ammon to help care for the sheep.

When they were in the field, some other Lamanites CHOSE to come and scatter the sheep so they could steal them. Ammon wanted to protect the sheep, but the king's other servants CHOSE to be afraid. So Ammon told them to gather the sheep while he CHOSE to defend them all. Ammon fought the robbers bravely. He CHOSE to risk his own life in order to save the sheep and the other servants.

When King Lamoni learned what Ammon had done, he was amazed. King Lamoni CHOSE to listen to Ammon's message about the gospel because he was impressed by Ammon's courage. In time, many of the Lamanites CHOSE to follow Jesus and join the Lord's Church.

APPLICATION

Divide the children up into four to six groups by their birthday months. If you have a large Primary, you may need more groups. Make sure there is at least one teacher in each group. Have the teachers help each child complete the sentence, "I will follow God's plan by choosing the right when I _____." Spend a few minutes in the groups discussing the importance of making good choices.

REVIEW

Talk about a time when you needed to make an important decision. How did you use the Lord's help to guide you? How have you seen His plan for you unfold in your life? Make sure the children understand how much Heavenly Father loves them and how His plan is meant to help them grow.

Chapter 3: March
Prophets Listen to Heavenly Father and Teach Us to Follow Him

MULTIMEDIA RESOURCES

"Follow the Prophet"—YouTube, LDS Youth, 4:16 (https://www.youtube.com/watch?v=AM8aBrgsxfg)

"He Lives: Testimonies of Jesus Christ"—YouTube, Mormon Channel, 2:09 (https://www.youtube.com/watch?v=9ddXNF29goo)

"We Need Living Prophets"—YouTube, Mormon Channel, 2:44 (https://www.youtube.com/watch?v=j8nSv95wXyM)

"Dare to Stand Alone"—YouTube, LDS Youth, 4:20 (https://www.youtube.com/watch?v=z_92mKlQOlk)

SONG LIST

Focus Song: "Stand for the Right" (159)

Additional songs: "Follow the Prophet" (110), "Latter-day Prophets" (134)

Review Songs: "If I Listen with My Heart," "I Will Follow God's Plan"

GOSPEL ART BOOK

"The Ten Commandments" (14)

Week 1: Heavenly Father Reveals Truth to Prophets

ATTENTION ACTIVITY

Have a leader or a child tell the story of the First Vision in his or her own words. (See Joseph Smith—History 1:14–20.) Or, alternatively, have a leader or an older child read aloud the lyrics to "Joseph Smith's First Prayer" (*Hymns*, 26).

SCRIPTURE

Amos 3:7

TALK

Enoch was a prophet who lived long ago. He had many glorious visions and taught the gospel to his people. All the people in his city were righteous. They called their city *Zion*. They looked forward to the time when Jesus would come. Because they were so good, Heavenly Father translated the whole city of Zion, meaning He took Zion up into heaven.

Because Enoch was a prophet, he learned lots of things about the future. Joseph Smith was also a prophet. He lived in our time—many, many years after Enoch and Zion were translated. By this time, most of the things we knew about Enoch had been forgotten or lost. Because Joseph was a prophet, he learned lots of things about the past.

Through revelation, Joseph Smith learned about Enoch and Zion. Then he taught the people about them. We are so blessed to have prophets in our time to learn the truth and share it with us.

LESSON

Discussion: Have the children hold up their scriptures. Point out that many of our favorite scriptures and scripture stories talk about a prophet. Many times, the prophet is the main person in the story. Explain that prophets have always led the Lord's true Church.

- Can you think of any prophets from the scriptures?
- What do prophets do that no one else can?

ACTIVITY

Help the children identify prophets from the scriptures by playing a matching game. Create two sets of index cards. On one set, write down the names of the prophets from the chart below (one name per card). On the other, write down the descriptions associated with those prophets. Mix the cards up, and then hand one card to each child. If you have more children than cards, you may need to have the children work in teams or pairs. If you have younger children, you will need to help them read their cards. Instruct the children to try to find the person whose card matches theirs. They will need to move quietly around the room to do this. When they are all paired up, have one person in each pair share the match with the rest of the group.

Prophet	Description
Adam	The first man on earth
Noah	Built an ark
Jacob	Had twelve sons
Moses	Led the people of Israel out of Egypt
Daniel	Was put into a den of lions
Malachi	Foretold the return of Elijah and the sealing powers
Nephi	Built a ship to take his family to the promised land
Alma the Younger	Saw an angel, who told him to repent
Samuel the Lamanite	Preached of Jesus's birth from the top of a wall
Moroni	Buried the Nephite records
Joseph Smith	Restored Christ's true Church
Brigham Young	Led the pioneers to the Salt Lake Valley

APPLICATION

Choose a few of the prophets from the activity and ask the children to explain how that prophet helped the people in his time to know what God wanted them to do. Examples: Moses spoke with God and recorded the Ten Commandments; Nephi prayed for help in the wilderness, and the Lord showed him how to build a ship; Joseph Smith translated the Book of Mormon and taught his people about temples, ordinances, and eternal families; Brigham Young led the pioneers to a new home in the West where God wanted them to settle.

REVIEW

Encourage the children to read about the prophets in the scriptures. Emphasize the importance of following their words and examples. Point out that some people in the scriptures did *not* follow the prophets and that these people were punished. Testify that we are blessed to have a modern prophet to guide us.

Week 2: Prophets Lead Us Back to Heavenly Father

ATTENTION ACTIVITY

Sing the song "Do As I'm Doing" (276). Invite a few children to take turns leading the group while the others follow the leader.

SCRIPTURE

D&C 107:91–92

TALK

Gideon has a little brother named Oliver and a little sister named Maggie. Because he's the oldest, Gideon knows it's important for him to set a good example for his brother and sister. He tries to teach them what he knows, like how to set the table, get ready for church, and clean up their toys when they're done playing. Gideon doesn't always remember to be a good example. And Oliver and Maggie don't always follow him. But they all love each other and try to obey their parents.

We all have an example we can follow: the prophet! The prophet is a man God has called to lead us and be our example. When we follow the prophet, we can find our way back to Jesus and Heavenly Father.

Long ago, some prophets in the scriptures led their people across oceans and open lands. Today, our prophet leads us spiritually and helps us make good choices. We can follow the prophet by listening to his words and trying to do what he says we should.

LESSON

Discussion: Show the children a compass or a picture of one. Explain that the needle on a compass always points in the same direction. Just like the needle always points the same way, a prophet always points us to God. When we follow the prophet, he will lead us to Heavenly Father.

- Who is our prophet today?
- How does he point us back to Heavenly Father?

ACTIVITY

Divide the children into their classes. Tell them that they will need to pay special attention to their teachers in this activity. Instruct the teachers to take their classes on a short walk outside (weather permitting) or inside the church building. Emphasize that the children need to be reverent on this walk and follow their teachers' examples.

APPLICATION

When the classes return, ask the children why it's important to follow a leader. Help them to understand that without a leader, we would likely all wander off in different directions. Some could get lost and others might not know which way to go.

REVIEW

Explain that Jesus knew we would need leaders in the Church. He has always called prophets to lead us. Throughout time, we can identify the Lord's Church by the fact that it is lead by a prophet, and the leader of all the prophets is Jesus Himself. Bear your testimony of the blessings that come when we follow the prophet.

Week 3: We Have a Living Prophet to Lead Us

ATTENTION ACTIVITY

Play sound clips from our modern prophets and Apostles. Have the children guess who the speaker is. The following address includes video testimonies with sound: https://www.lds.org/prophets-and-apostles/what-are-prophets-testimonies?lang=eng&cid=PA0414.

(You may need to download each video ahead of time or check to be sure that they will stream at church.)

SCRIPTURE

Ephesians 2:19–20

TALK

Maack is excited for general conference! Last time, he got to play with his brother and sisters while his parents watched conference on their computer. He drew pictures of the things the speakers were saying and listened carefully when the prophet spoke. This time, Maack is even more excited about conference because he gets to attend a session in the Conference Center with his grandparents. He can't wait to see the prophet in person and hear the choir singing.

Conference is a special time for all of us. Whether we watch the sessions on computers or TVs, or we listen on the Internet or the radio, there is something special about conference weekend. It is a time for us to be with our friends and families and listen to the words of our Church leaders. You don't have to attend conference in person to know that the words you hear are true. All you have to do is listen carefully, and then pray.

If you pay close attention, Heavenly Father will help you learn answers to your questions during conference. It is a good time to build your testimony and receive revelation.

LESSON

Discussion: Remind the children that prophets are our link to Heavenly Father. And while we have personal revelation to guide us, when Heavenly Father wants to reveal something to His entire Church, He tells the prophet first. The prophet relays this information to us.

Time to Share

- How can we find out what the prophet has told us lately?
- Can you think of some examples of specific counsel that prophets have given us in the latter days?

ACTIVITY

Tell the children you want them to continue thinking about specific items of counsel our modern prophets have given us in recent years. Ask for a volunteer to draw a picture of one of the following items, without speaking. Have the other children guess what the first child is drawing. Invite the first child who guesses correctly to either draw the next item or choose someone else to do so.

- Keep a journal
- Don't wear more than one pair of earrings
- Help with family history work
- Study the scriptures
- Fast and pray
- Go to the temple
- Obey the Word of Wisdom
- Pay tithing
- Listen to and watch only uplifting music and media
- Learn as much as you can
- Strengthen and defend the family

You may need to offer hints or explanations because some of these concepts may be too complex for young children.

APPLICATION

Encourage the children to choose one of the items of counsel that you discussed in the lesson and work on obeying the prophet's counsel in that area for the next week or two. Have them share ideas with those sitting next to them or with their teachers.

REVIEW

Tell the children that sustaining the prophet is an important part of being a member of our Church. Share with them any experiences you have had that have helped you to know our prophet is a man chosen by God to lead us in our time. Encourage them to pray to know this for themselves. Then invite them to sustain the prophet by listening carefully to his counsel and trying to obey his words.

Week 4: Following the Prophet Keeps Me Safe

ATTENTION ACTIVITY

Invite a class of children to act out the story of Moses healing his people in the wilderness when they looked upon his staff. (See Numbers 21:8–9; Alma 33:19–22.)

SCRIPTURE

Ezekiel 33:7

TALK

Jenna and McKenzie love to ride their bikes. They like to ride to the park and all around their neighborhood. Their parents want them to have fun on their bikes, but they also want them to obey the rules. The girls know that they should never ride without their helmets. They also know that they need to obey traffic rules, signal when they want to turn, and watch out for cars.

When Jenna and McKenzie ride their bikes, the rules are there to help them be safe. Disobeying the rules could mean getting hurt or getting in an accident.

Our prophet tells us the rules we need to follow to stay spiritually safe. These rules are called commandments. Sometimes we are tempted to disobey the commandments or ignore them for a little while. But we need to remember that the rules that our prophet gives us aren't just suggestions or good ideas. They are much more important than that.

If we always follow the prophet and the commandments he gives us from Heavenly Father, we can be safe and stay spiritually strong.

LESSON

Discussion: Tell the children the story of the prophet Elijah and the widow of Zarephath (1 Kings 17:8–16).

- What might have happened if the widow had not obeyed Elijah?
- How did she know that Elijah was a prophet? (See verse 9.)

This woman had to choose between following the prophet and taking care of her son. But because she chose to follow the prophet's instructions, she was able to save herself, her son, and Elijah.

Time to Share

ACTIVITY

Pass out papers and crayons to the children. On the board, write, "The prophet tells us to _____" and also, "The prophet tells us not to _____."

On one side of their papers, have the children draw a picture of something the prophet has told us we should do. On the other side, have them draw a picture of something he has warned us we should not do.

APPLICATION

The scriptures tell us that once the prophets have warned us, we need to warn others as well. Have the children help you think of some things the prophet has warned us against. They can use the same things they illustrated for the second half of the activity. With older children, you may want to write these warnings on the board. Then ask each child to pick one of the warnings you mentioned and choose someone to warn about that thing. The children can choose to warn a friend, a family member, or someone else. It does not matter if the person they choose has heard the warning before because we all need reminders to follow the prophet.

REVIEW

Express gratitude for prophets—both those we read about in the scriptures and our modern prophets. Share an experience you or someone in your family had when following the prophet kept you safe or helped you accomplish a difficult task. Encourage the children to always follow the prophet so they can be safe and happy.

Chapter 4: April
Jesus Lived and Died for Me

MULTIMEDIA RESOURCES

"Who Is Jesus Christ? A 60-Second Overview"—YouTube, mormon. org, 1:23 (https://www.youtube.com/watch?v=MTkzx1K5NHU)

"Calming the Tempest"—YouTube, Mormon Channel, 2:17 (https://www.youtube.com/watch?v=hj0cVBYKaEg)

"The Feeding of the 5000"—YouTube, Mormon Channel, 2:52 (https://www.youtube.com/watch?v=UtrjViTgPHs)

"Jesus Is Baptized by John"—YouTube, Mormon Channel, 2:54 (https://www.youtube.com/watch?v=9_dr9njVzKM)

"Sermon on the Mount: Treasures in Heaven"—YouTube, Mormon Channel, 4:32 (https://www.youtube.com/watch?v=-3nN9-C1yKU)

SONG LIST

Focus Song: "Praise to the Man" (27)

Additional Songs: "He Sent His Son" (34), "The Third Article of Faith" (123), "Jesus Once Was a Little Child" (55)

Review Songs: "If I Listen with My Heart," "I Will Follow God's Plan," "Stand for the Right"

GOSPEL ART BOOK

"Jesus Washing the Apostles' Feet" (55)

Week 1: Jesus Was Foreordained to Save Us

ATTENTION ACTIVITY

Write the question, "What is your earliest memory?" on the board. Say it out loud for the younger children. Give the children a moment or two to reflect. Then have a few come to the front of the room and share their answers, or simply have each child share with those he or she is sitting next to.

SCRIPTURE

Abraham 3:27

TALK

Harrison loves to play peek-a-boo with his little sister, Harper. Sometimes he uses his hands to cover his face and other times he uses a blanket to cover his whole body. When Harrison is under the blanket, he can't see what's going on around him. He can't see his mommy making dinner or his daddy working on the computer. His family can't see him either, but they still know that he's there because they can see the blanket. When Harrison pops out again and says, "Peek-a-boo!" they all laugh, especially Harper.

Sometimes it seems like we have a blanket covering our minds. Even though we lived with Heavenly Father before we were born, we can't remember that. Heavenly Father sent us to earth without those memories so that we could choose for ourselves how we would live. After we die, it will be like coming out from underneath the blanket. We will be able to remember what happened before we were born and see our families again, including Heavenly Father.

Even though our minds are covered right now, we need to remember that there is more going on than what we can see underneath our blankets. That is what it means to have an eternal perspective—to think about all the things that we cannot see now but that make a big difference in our lives before and after we live on earth.

LESSON

Discussion: Remind the children of the attention activity (if you used it) and ask them to think about their memories.

- What happened before those memories?
- Where were we before we were born?
- What did we do there?

Explain that before birth, we lived with our Heavenly Father. He presented a plan to us. Heavenly Father knew that we would try our best but that we were not perfect. We would need a perfect person to sacrifice Himself for us so that we could come back to Heavenly Father. Jesus said He would die for us.

ACTIVITY

Create a storyboard that tells the story of the grand council in heaven. Divide the children into six groups and assign each group one of the following events. Have them read their assigned scripture(s) together, and then draw a picture to illustrate that event.

When the groups are finished, invite them up to the front of the room, in order, to present their part of the story.

1. Heavenly Father presented a plan for us to grow and become like Him. As part of the plan, we needed a Savior (Moses 1:39; see also Abraham 3:22).
2. Satan said he would save everyone, but he wanted to force people to do right and keep all of the glory for himself (Moses 4:1).
3. Jesus said He would follow Heavenly Father's plan and sacrifice Himself (Abraham 3:24–26).
4. All of us had to choose if we would follow Jesus or Satan. Many spirits (about one third) chose to follow Satan. They did not get to come to earth or receive a body. Instead, they were cast out of heaven (D&C 29:36–37).
5. The rest of us chose to follow Jesus. We were excited to get bodies and to learn new things here on earth (Job 38:4–7).
6. Now that we are here, we still need to follow Jesus, and not Satan, so that we can return to live with Heavenly Father (2 Nephi 2:27).

APPLICATION

How does knowing that we chose Jesus before we were born help us to continue following Him now? Remind the children of what it means to have an eternal perspective and encourage them to make good choices throughout the week so they can continue to follow the Lord's plan. If time permits, ask them to talk about the good choices they want to make in the coming week.

REVIEW

Testify of the happiness that can come to us when we follow the plan of redemption. Explain that each one of us made good choices before we came to earth, that we fought for what was right. Tell the children how important it is to keep fighting for righteousness here on the earth and to share what we know about this plan with others around us.

Week 2: Jesus Is Our Perfect Example

ATTENTION ACTIVITY

Invite two children to the front of the room. Have them face each other. Tell one child to act as the leader and perform a few simple actions like reaching up high, stretching out with his or her arms wide, and so on. The other child should try to copy the first one as closely as possible, like a mirror image. Help the children remain reverent during this activity.

SCRIPTURE

3 Nephi 18:16

TALK

John the Baptist was Jesus's cousin. John lived in the desert by himself. Lots of people came to see him and hear him teach. John baptized these people and told them that soon an even greater leader would come to show them the way. This greater leader was Jesus Christ.

One day, Jesus came to see John. Jesus asked John to baptize Him. At first, John was confused. He knew that Jesus was perfect and didn't need to be baptized. But Jesus explained that He came to be baptized to set an example for His followers—including us! Jesus wanted all of His disciples to know how important it is to be baptized.

We all need to be baptized like Jesus was. And we need to follow His example in other ways too. Jesus didn't get angry when people laughed at Him or hurt Him. Instead, He prayed for those people. We should do the same thing. Jesus was kind, so we should be kind. Jesus served others, so we should serve those around us. When we follow Jesus's example, we can return to live with Him forever.

LESSON

Discussion: Remind the children that in the previous month, we discussed how prophets can be good examples for us. Then ask them who the prophet could look to for an example. Explain that Jesus is an example everyone can look up to because He is the only perfect person to ever live on earth.

- What does it mean to be perfect?

Time to Share

ACTIVITY

Display several pictures of Jesus from the *Gospel Art Book* around the room (see list below). Have the children turn in their chairs or walk around to the different pictures to see them as you discuss them. If you do not have access to the *Gospel Art Book*, either in print or online, you may choose to take the children for a walk around the church building to look at any pictures of Jesus on the walls. For each picture, ask them:

- Who is in this picture?
- What is Jesus doing?
- What could we do to follow Jesus's example in this way?

Suggested *Gospel Art Book* pictures
- "Jesus Praying with His Mother" (33)
- "Boy Jesus in the Temple" (34)
- "John the Baptist Baptizing Jesus" (35)
- "Christ Healing the Sick at Bethesda" (42)
- "The Ten Lepers" (46)
- "Jesus Cleansing the Temple" (51)
- "Jesus Washing the Apostles' Feet" (55)
- "Jesus Carrying a Lost Lamb" (64)
- "Jesus at the Door" (65)

APPLICATION

Read 3 Nephi 12:48 and identify who is speaking. Ask younger children to think of ways they could follow Christ's example and try to be more perfect. Ask older children why they think Christ commanded us to be perfect when He knew that we would sin. Discuss how Christ can help us overcome our weaknesses and turn them into strengths (see Ether 12:27) and how our ultimate perfection will not come in this life.

REVIEW

Help the children understand that while Jesus wants us to make good choices, He knows that we will make mistakes. That's why He helped Heavenly Father enact a plan that lets us repent and be good again. He is more concerned with the direction we are going than with how close we are to perfection. Share your thoughts about following Christ's example and trying to become perfect.

Week 3: Jesus Died So I Could Repent

ATTENTION ACTIVITY

Display a clean white piece of paper. Invite one child to draw on the paper with a red marker, then ask the other children if they can change the paper back to white again. Read and explain Isaiah 1:18. You could encourage older children to memorize this verse or help them to memorize it as part of your lesson, if time permits.

SCRIPTURE

Articles of Faith 1:3

TALK

When Sadie moved to a new town, she had to go to a different school. She didn't know anyone there, and it was scary to meet so many new people. Sadie felt like she was all alone. Her parents encouraged her to make friends, but Sadie just wanted to go back to her old town with her old friends.

Then her older brother Jake told her something that could help. He explained that Sadie could use the Atonement to help her not feel sad and to give her the courage she needed to make new friends. Jake said that when Jesus Christ sacrificed Himself for us, He made it so that we could become better.

Sometimes we use the Atonement to repent—and we all need to do that. But other times, we can use the Atonement to become better or not feel sad. Any time you need to use the Atonement, you can pray, and Heavenly Father and Jesus will bless you with the power you need.

LESSON

Discussion: Have the children imagine their favorite dessert. Ask a few of them to share the treats they're imagining. Tell them to pretend to eat some. Then have them pretend that this same dessert is covered with slimy mud and dirt. Ask them if they would still want to eat it.

Explain that when we sin, we take something good and turn it into something dirty or sad. Instead of making a good choice and getting closer to Heavenly Father, we choose to get closer to Satan. Tell the children that Jesus knew we would sin. He performed the Atonement for us so that we could change from bad to good.

- What does the word *Atonement* mean?
- How can we use the Atonement to change?

ACTIVITY

Practice repenting by learning to say sorry and being willing to forgive. Pair the children up with the person sitting next to them. Have them decide which person should be first and which person should be second. Read the following story:

One time, two friends were playing together at the park. When the second friend had to leave, the first friend helped pick up the toys they had been playing with. Under the slide, the first friend saw a really cool toy that belonged to the second friend. The first friend wanted to keep this toy, so the first friend hid it back under the slide. After the second friend left, the first friend went back to get the toy and play with it.

- What should the first friend do? (Return the toy and apologize.)
- How would you feel if you were the second friend?

Have the children act out what should happen next. The first child in each pair should apologize and the second child should forgive.

Now read this next story: One time, two friends were playing soccer against each other. The second friend tried to shoot a goal, but the ball did not go in. However, the first friend thought it did. The second friend decided to go along with it because the second friend wanted to win.

- What should the second friend do to make things right? (Tell the truth and apologize.)
- How would you react in this situation if you were the first friend?

Again, have the children act out what should happen next.

APPLICATION

Ask the children to reflect on the choices they have made in the past day or two. See if they can think of any times when they should have made a good choice, but they made a bad one instead. Encourage them to use the Atonement to repent by apologizing if necessary and trying to make things right.

REVIEW

Explain to the children that the Atonement fixes everything. It can help us fix our sins when we need to repent. It can also help fix feelings of sadness, fear, loneliness, or frustration. Through the Atonement, we can become better people than we would be on our own. Encourage them to think of ways to rely on the Savior and use the Atonement more frequently in their lives.

Week 4: Jesus Lived Again, and I Will Too

ATTENTION ACTIVITY

Bring a sheet with you and invite two teachers to hold it up in front of the children. Invite a few children to come up (one at a time), walk behind the sheet for a moment, and then step back out so the rest of the children can see them again. Explain that when we die, we are not really gone. We still exist in another place, where we work and wait. Then when we are resurrected we will have our bodies again. Jesus Christ made this process possible.

This activity could also be done by having the children step out through a door into the hallway, and then back in through the door.

SCRIPTURE

John 11:25

TALK

Milo loves his great-grandmother. When Milo was younger, they liked to play board games together. And when they finished, she always gave him a big scoop of ice cream. Now his great-grandmother is too old to play with him. Instead, she has to stay in bed all day. Milo knows she doesn't feel well and that one day in the next few months, she will pass away. His family prays for her to not be in pain.

Even though Milo will miss her, he knows his great-grandmother will be happier after she dies. She will be with her husband, Milo's great-grandfather, who passed away before Milo was born. And because their family has been sealed together in the temple. Milo knows he will see his great-grandmother again, and they will be a family forever.

When we die, we are separated from our bodies for a little while. This happened to Jesus too. But three days after He died, Jesus rose from the dead. He was the first one to be resurrected. His spirit and body came together again. He showed us all that death is not the end. It is just another step on our way back to our Heavenly Father.

LESSON

Discussion: As part of Heavenly Father's plan, we know that our time on earth will end. But emphasize that death is not an ending. It is the beginning of a new part of our eternal progression. Explain that Jesus made it possible for us to be resurrected.

- What does it mean to be resurrected?
- What happens to our bodies after we die?
- What happens to our spirits after we die?

ACTIVITY

Bring a flashlight and a lamp with you. Explain to the children that after we die and are resurrected, there are three different degrees of glory, or three different kingdoms, in which we can go to live and stay for eternity.

Tell the children that the first is called the telestial kingdom. Turn off the lights in the room and turn on the flashlight. (Note: This activity will work best if you can also close any curtains in your room. However, you may also need to be sensitive to any children who are afraid of the dark.)

Explain to the children that the glory of the telestial kingdom is like the little bit of light from the stars, or from your flashlight. Heavenly Father and Jesus cannot visit there, but the people there will be able to feel the Holy Ghost sometimes.

Turn on the lamp. Explain to the children that the second kingdom is called the terrestrial kingdom. Its glory is like the moon, or like the light from the lamp. Jesus can visit there, but Heavenly Father cannot.

Then turn all of the lights in the room back on, but turn the lamp and flashlight off. Explain that the third kingdom is the celestial kingdom. This is where we want to go. In the celestial kingdom, we can live with Heavenly Father and Jesus Christ. It is a beautiful place where we will be happy.

Turn on the lamp and flashlight again in addition to the lights in the room. Explain that the highest degree of glory in the celestial kingdom is the best place for us. If we are righteous and sealed in the temple, we will be able to live with our families there and continue learning and growing forever.

APPLICATION

Have the children draw pictures of the celestial kingdom. Encourage them to include their families, along with Heavenly Father and Jesus

Time to Share

Christ, in the picture. Let them take the picture home to show their families. Be sensitive to those children whose family members are not members or are not active—or those children whose family situations are complicated in any way—but explain that if we try to always be righteous, Heavenly Father will bless us and that every family can be a forever family.

REVIEW

Bear your testimony to the children that Jesus was resurrected, and we will be too. Help them understand how grateful you are for your knowledge of the resurrection. Share with them your thoughts about life after death and our Heavenly Father's plan.

Chapter 5: May
Joseph Smith Restored the True Church

MULTIMEDIA RESOURCES

"Mormon Church: The Message of the Restoration"—YouTube, Mormon Channel, 2:22 (https://www.youtube.com/watch?v=ySyv1I 2e9RE)

"The Gospel Restored"—YouTube, Joseph Smith Papers, 3:59 (https://www.youtube.com/watch?v=nr1h2NbV6OQ)

"Praise to the Man (Music Video) - Mormon Tabernacle Choir"— YouTube, Mormon Tabernacle Choir, 6:16 (https://www.youtube.com/ watch?v=LeXrjFgNPTc)

"Book of Mormon Stories (1/54): Joseph Smith sees a vision of God and Jesus Christ"—YouTube, Mormon Channel, 2:56 (https://www. youtube.com/watch?v=FMQEb9A9L2g)

SONG LIST

Focus Song: "Praise to the Man" (27)

Additional Songs: "The Golden Plates" (86), "On a Golden Springtime" (88)

Review Songs: "If I Listen with My Heart," "I Will Follow God's Plan," "Stand for the Right"

GOSPEL ART BOOK

"The First Vision" (90)

Week 1: The Truth Has Been Restored

ATTENTION ACTIVITY

Ask one or two children to come to the front of the room and talk about something that is special to them. It could be a favorite toy or a family keepsake. (If you have time during the previous week, you might call a few children ahead of time and ask them to bring their favorite thing with them as show and tell.) When each child finishes, ask

- How would you feel if you lost this object?
- What if someone found it and brought it back to you after you thought it was lost? How would you feel then?

Explain that today's lesson will focus on something very precious that was lost—the Lord's true Church—and how Joseph Smith helped restore it in our time.

SCRIPTURE

James 1:5

TALK

Joseph Smith was a curious young man. When he was young, he wanted to know the truth. He tried to find answers to his questions in the Bible. He asked his family and friends what they thought was right and he talked to the leaders of the different churches in his town to see what they had to say. But some of them told him one thing was true, and others told him that something else was right. After a while Joseph became so confused by the different answers he heard that he didn't know what to think. He wanted to choose the right church, but he didn't know how to find it.

One day, he read a scripture in the Bible that told him if he was confused or needed to know the truth, he could pray and ask the Lord. Joseph thought this was a great idea. He chose to say his prayer out in the woods near his house. When Joseph prayed and asked to know which church was right, Heavenly Father and Jesus Christ appeared to him.

They told him that none of the churches were right. Instead, Joseph would need to begin a new church, one that had the same kinds of people and the same priesthood power that Jesus used in His true Church.

As Joseph grew older, he had many more visions and learned many things by the Spirit. With the help of Jesus and Heavenly Father, Joseph Smith restored Jesus's true Church to the earth—the same Church Jesus had in His day, and the same one we have now.

LESSON

Discussion: Tell the children that after Jesus and His Apostles died, the true Church slowly faded away. The people did not know how to organize themselves and, more important, the priesthood power was lost. The scriptures were changed, and everyone was confused. Hundreds of years later, Heavenly Father and Jesus Christ visited Joseph Smith. They knew that it was the right time to restore the true Church and the priesthood power to the earth.

- What does it mean to restore something?

Show the children a picture of something that has been restored. You might choose the Provo Tabernacle, which was restored as a temple after being nearly destroyed by a fire. You could show the children a photo of what the tabernacle looked like right after the fire and what it looks like now.

ACTIVITY

On a piece of poster board, write the sixth article of faith and cut the poster board into six puzzle pieces. (You may also choose to make a puzzle out of a picture of a temple or something similar.) Have the children help you assemble the puzzle by doing the following activity. Sing "The Sixth Article of Faith" together. Then ask a volunteer to recite the sixth article of faith. You may want to let the children volunteer in small groups or have them ask a teacher for help at first. If the children can successfully repeat the article of faith, have one of them come to the front of the room, choose a puzzle piece and place it where it belongs. You will probably want to tape the pieces to the board so that all the children can see the puzzle. Sing the song again as a review and repeat this process until the puzzle is complete.

APPLICATION

For each of the roles that are named in the sixth article of faith, ask the children if they know who fills that role today. Talk about the things

Time to Share

each of these people or groups do for the Church and help the children understand their relationship to that person or group.

- Apostles
- prophet
- pastor (bishop)
- teachers
- evangelist (patriarch)

REVIEW

Show the children the completed puzzle from the activity, and then explain that each piece needed to come together in the right way to form the puzzle correctly. When the Church was restored, we also needed to have all of the pieces just the right way so that it would follow the pattern Jesus established when He was on the earth. Express to the children that you are grateful for the fulness of the gospel, the organization of the Church, and the truths we have learned through the Restoration.

Week 2: Joseph Smith Helped Restore Jesus's Church

ATTENTION ACTIVITY

Watch "What the Restoration Means for Me - The Apostasy and the Restoration" (YouTube, Mormon Channel, 4:44 [https://www.youtube.com/watch?v=gcKgxTUZtEk]).

SCRIPTURE

D&C 110:1

TALK

Samantha's grandfather likes to restore furniture. That means he takes an old piece of furniture and makes it like new again. Samantha loves watching her grandfather work in his shop. One time, he brought home a smelly old dresser that was covered with dust and spiderwebs. Some of the drawers were missing, and the mirror on top was cracked. Samantha thought it looked like junk.

But she watched as her grandfather carefully cleaned, sanded, and stained the dresser. He put a new mirror on top and built new drawers to replace the ones that were missing. Then he replaced all the knobs and handles with shiny new ones. It took him several days, but when he was done, the dresser looked beautiful—maybe even better than it had when it was brand new.

Joseph Smith helped restore the Church in the same way that Samantha's grandfather restores furniture. When Joseph began the Church, many people were confused about Jesus. Through revelation, Joseph made everything clear again. The Lord showed him truths that were missing. Now our Church is the same as the one Jesus created in His day.

LESSON

Discussion: Explain to the children that during his time as prophet, Joseph Smith revealed many truths. He restored the fulness of the gospel for our time.

- What does it mean to have the fulness of the gospel?
- Do you remember what kinds of things were restored?

Time to Share

Ask the children to help you list these things on the board. Your answers may include the following: temple ordinances; the doctrine of eternal families and the plan of salvation; baptism by immersion; the gift of the Holy Ghost; the Word of Wisdom; priesthood powers, keys, and ordinances; the organization of the Church; the Book of Mormon; the concept of continuing revelation; truths about the Godhead; a new translation of the Bible; the Pearl of Great Price; and so on. Keep this list on the board to use later on in the lesson.

ACTIVITY

Create a Restoration treasure hunt. Invite four teachers or leaders to help you with this activity. Have three of them stand in three corners of the room. Print or show them the second, third, and fourth clues listed below. You will stand in the first corner with the first clue. Have the fourth teacher stand in the hallway, just outside the door, with the treasure.

Tell the children that they are going to go on a treasure hunt to find the truth. Explain that when Joseph Smith wanted to know the truth about something, he had to study it in his mind, and then ask Heavenly Father if it was right. By doing this, he was able to restore the Lord's true Church, one piece at a time—learning line upon line.

Give the children a clue about something that was restored by Joseph Smith. They can study the clue and talk to others about it. Then, when they think they know the answer, they can ask you and see if they are right. If they are, they can go to the next teacher and get their next clue. When they have solved all four clues, they can step out into the hallway and get their treasure.

Clues for Younger Children	Answer
This is a special place where we go to feel the Spirit.	The temple
This power comes from Heavenly Father to bless us.	The priesthood
This tells us stories that teach us about people in the Americas long ago.	The Book of Mormon
This is a commandment from God about how to care for our bodies.	The Word of Wisdom

Give the older children both the clue and the scripture reference. Have them work in small groups, or with their teachers if needed, to find the scriptures, read them, and solve the clues.

Clues for Older Children	Scripture Reference	Answer
The early Church members built a special place. What was the place, and what would it be used for?	D&C 109:1–5	The Kirtland Temple was built for the Son of Man to visit.
Two men were given something precious. Who were the men and what was the gift?	Joseph Smith—History 1:66–69	The Prophet Joseph and Oliver Cowdery had the Aaronic Priesthood bestowed upon them.
A special record was kept for "a wise purpose." What was the record and why was it kept?	1 Nephi 9:5 (see also D&C 10:1, 38–42)	Small plates of Nephi were written because the Lord knew Joseph and Martin Harris would end up losing the first 116 pages of the Book of Mormon translation.
Four promises were given to those who would obey a commandment. What was this commandment, and what were the promises?	D&C 89:1–3, 18–21	The Word of Wisdom is the commandment, and those who obey it are promised health, wisdom, energy, and that the destroying angel will pass them by.

Bring a small prize or treat to hand out to the children as their treasure. It could be as simple as a sticker, a piece of paper with a favorite scripture printed on it, a photo of a temple, or a picture of Joseph Smith that they can take home to color.

Note that some children may complete this activity faster than others. Help those who finish quickly to remain reverent by having the pianist play Primary songs in the background as the other children finish. Or you may choose to show a video to the children who finish early (see suggested list in the multimedia resources at the beginning of the chapter).

APPLICATION

Have the children take turns standing up and sharing why they are grateful for the Restoration by completing this sentence with one of the answers you listed on the board earlier: "I am grateful Joseph Smith helped to restore _____ [fill in an answer from the board], because _____ [have the children tell why they are grateful]."

REVIEW

Invite the children to thank Heavenly Father for Joseph Smith in their prayers that week. Help them understand that the Church will never again be taken from the earth and that we need to live true to the things that we know. Share with them how blessed we are to have the fulness of the gospel in our time.

Week 3: The Book of Mormon Is for Our Day

ATTENTION ACTIVITY

Have the children play a guessing game. Tell them you're thinking of a Book of Mormon prophet and have them ask you yes or no questions until they guess who it is. You may wish to give them a clue to start. If they guess too quickly, play the game again with a different prophet.

SCRIPTURE

Mormon 8:35

TALK

Mormon was a prophet who lived long ago. Heavenly Father gave him the job of reading all the Nephite records that had been written over a thousand years. After he read them, Mormon needed to put them all together into one set of plates. He worked for a long time, engraving symbols on the plates. Then, when he was done, he gave the plates to his son, Moroni.

Heavenly Father gave Moroni the job of writing a little more on the plates, and then burying them in the ground. Mormon and Moroni were some of the last Nephites. Moroni saw all of the other Nephites get destroyed. That's why he wanted to take good care of their records, so that someday when the time was right, someone would find the plates, learn about the Nephites, and tell their story again.

Mormon and Moroni worked hard to do the jobs Heavenly Father gave them. They knew that if they obeyed Heavenly Father, He would make sure the Nephites weren't forgotten forever. Even though the Nephites were destroyed, their record survived. When we read the Book of Mormon, we can remember the Nephites and all of the righteous prophets who kept records for us to read someday.

LESSON

Discussion: Explain to the children that before Joseph Smith could help restore the Church, the Lord needed him to be ready. That's why He sent the angel Moroni to visit Joseph every year for four years. At the end of the four years, Joseph received the gold plates. He was now ready to translate the Book of Mormon and start the true Church.

Time to Share

- Why was Moroni, and not another prophet, sent to visit Joseph?
- What kinds of things do you think Joseph needed to learn before he could translate the Book of Mormon?

ACTIVITY

Have the younger children illustrate a picture of Moroni visiting Joseph Smith for the first time. Display picture 91 in the *Gospel Art Book*, "Moroni Appears to Joseph Smith in His Room," as a guide.

Have older children pretend to translate. Write the letter substitution code (see below) on the board and print out the following coded scripture for them. Alternatively, you may decide to write the scripture on the board as well and work on decoding it as a group.

Scripture

KQS NR IFD VGZDO GM IFD FGPR XFGCI RD JKR UQGZ IFD IOWIF GM KPP IFTQXC.—JGOGQT 10:5

(Answer: And by the power of the Holy Ghost ye may know the truth of all things.—Moroni 10:5)

A	B	D	E	F	G	H	I	K	L
K	*N*	*S*	*D*	*M*	*X*	*F*	*T*	*U*	*P*

M	N	O	P	R	S	T	U	W	Y
J	*Q*	*G*	*V*	*O*	*C*	*I*	*W*	*Z*	*R*

APPLICATION

Help the children understand just how much time Joseph Smith sacrificed to translate the Book of Mormon and the personal danger he was in while he had the gold plates. Encourage them to think of ways they could sacrifice to spread the gospel, learn more from the scriptures, or build up the Lord's kingdom. Brainstorm some ideas with them and write them on the board for older children. Then sing "We'll Bring the World His Truth" (*Hymns*, 172).

REVIEW

Share your testimony of the Book of Mormon, and tell the children that they can pray and learn the truth of it for themselves. Explain that without Joseph Smith and all of the prophets who kept the records faithfully, we would not know about the Nephites and the things they learned about Jesus. We are blessed to have the Book of Mormon.

Week 4: We Have the Power of God on the Earth Again

ATTENTION ACTIVITY

Have a few children come up to the front and act out the restoration of the Aaronic Priesthood (see Joseph Smith—History 1:68–72).

SCRIPTURE

Moroni 10:7

TALK

One time there was a big storm near Maddie and Eli's house. The wind and rain were so strong that it was too dangerous to go outside and play. Then the power went out. When it got dark, they had to use flashlights. They couldn't cook any food in the microwave, and their whole family had to sleep downstairs near the fireplace, where it was warm.

It was a little bit like camping, but Maddie and Eli were worried about how their friends and neighbors were doing in the storm. When the power came back on after a few days, they were so grateful to be able to sleep in their own beds again and turn on the lights whenever they needed to.

The priesthood is another kind of power. It is the power of God. Joseph Smith received the priesthood from heavenly messengers who visited him and brought the power back to the earth. For a long time, the people on earth did not have this power. It was like they were living in the dark. Now that we have the priesthood again, we use it to heal the sick, perform sacred ordinances, and seal families together for all eternity. We are so blessed to have the power of God on the earth again.

LESSON

Discussion: If you did not use the attention activity, review the story of the restoration of the Aaronic Priesthood in your own words (see Joseph Smith—History 1:68–72).

- Why did the priesthood need to be restored?
- Who came to restore the priesthood?
- Who gave John the Baptist the authority to restore the priesthood?

Time to Share

ACTIVITY

Have the children form a chain by standing up and holding hands or linking arms. Depending on how many children you have, you may need to form two or three different chains. Carefully move the entire chain around the room in one direction, and then another. What happens when children unlink their arms or drop their hands? Is the chain still connected? What if the chain moved while someone wasn't linked to it? Would that person still move? What about all the people behind the unlinked person?

When all of the children have returned to their seats, explain that the priesthood connects us to God. It is His power, and it must be given from one person to the next by proper authority. After Jesus and His Apostles died, there was no one left to carry on the chain, and our connection to Heavenly Father's power was lost.

APPLICATION

Have the children create paperclip chain necklaces or bracelets to remind them of how priesthood lines link us to Heavenly Father. Ask them to share any experiences they have had when the priesthood blessed their lives or brought them closer to Heavenly Father (such as a father's blessing, being baptized, a healing blessing, and so on).

REVIEW

Share with the children an experience you had in which the priesthood blessed your life. Testify that it is the power of God on the earth and express how grateful you are that Heavenly Father and Joseph Smith restored the priesthood.

Chapter 6: June
The First Principles and Ordinances of the Gospel Help Me Return to Heavenly Father

MULTIMEDIA RESOURCES

"Pure and Simple Faith"—YouTube, Mormon Channel, 5:30 (https://www.youtube.com/watch?v=TDdde1Pi1lU)

"The Sting of the Scorpion"—YouTube, LDS Youth, 2:50 (https://www.youtube.com/watch?v=XZCQHPGT78o)

"The Road to Damascus - Saul Takes His Journey"—YouTube, Mormon Channel, 5:21 (https://www.youtube.com/watch?v=uPlez-rwhKY)

"Jesus Is Baptized by John"—YouTube, Mormon Channel, 2:54 (https://www.youtube.com/watch?v=9_dr9njVzKM)

"Feeling the Holy Ghost: Power of the Holy Spirit"—YouTube, Mormon Channel, 3:17 (https://www.youtube.com/watch?v=xc6TQ0Ej-BY)

SONG LIST

Focus Song: "I Love to See the Temple" (95)

Additional Songs: "The Fourth Article of Faith" (124), "Baptism" (100), "Faith" (96), "Listen, Listen" (107)

Review Songs: "If I Listen with My Heart," "I Will Follow God's Plan," "Stand for the Right," "Praise to the Man"

GOSPEL ART BOOK

"Girl Being Baptized" (104)

Week 1: Faith Is the First Principle

ATTENTION ACTIVITY

Read Hebrews 11:1–32 (or a portion) aloud. Instruct the children to stand up any time they hear the word *faith*.

SCRIPTURE

Alma 32:21

TALK

Adam loves his science class in school. In science, he is learning about gravity, which is the force that pulls something down to earth. When you drop something, gravity makes it fall down instead of flying away. Adam knows that gravity is a true principle because he can do experiments and observe it. For example, he could drop something and measure how quickly it falls.

But Adam also knows that there are some things that are true that can't be measured by science. These are things that Adam can't hear with his ears, see with his eyes, feel with his hands, taste with his tongue, or smell with his nose. In other words, they are eternal principles that our bodies can't observe or sense. But our spirits can!

The way we learn these principles is by a different sort of experiment. We use faith. Alma taught that when we experiment with our faith, even just a little bit, our spirits can observe and learn things that our bodies cannot know for certain. That is how we gain a testimony. Adam knows that if he experiments with his faith, he can gain a testimony of his own. All he needs to do is nurture his faith.

LESSON

Discussion: Ask the children how they know that their parents love them. Explain that love is not something we can see or hear. It's something we feel with our hearts. There are many ways to show others you love them, but you cannot force them to feel your love. It's something they have to choose for themselves.

Explain that faith is the same. It's not something we see or hear. It's something we feel with our hearts. Even though we can use our faith to do amazing things, we cannot force someone to have faith or believe. Like love, faith is something we have to choose for ourselves.

ACTIVITY

Bring a small bag with sixteen pebbles or marbles in it. Empty the contents of the bag onto a table. Explain to the children that the pebbles represent the sixteen stones that the brother of Jared took to the Lord, and that the object of this activity is to get all of the pebbles back into the bag.

Tell the following story about the brother of Jared. Explain that he had to exercise his faith many times to keep his friends and family safe and bring them to the promised land. At each break in the story, call on a child to answer the question about faith. If the child answers correctly, have the child come to the front of the room and put two of the pebbles back into the bag. If the answer is incorrect, invite another child to answer and add the pebbles. Note that some of these questions may be too advanced for young children. You will likely need to offer hints or suggestions for them. Use your best judgment to adapt this activity to the needs of your children.

Story

Jared and his brother lived a long, long time ago. In their day, many people wanted to build a tower to get to heaven. The brother of Jared knew this was not right. He did not need a tower to know that heaven existed.

- *How exactly did the brother of Jared know that heaven was real if he couldn't see it? (Answer: He had faith.)*

Heavenly Father needed to stop these people before they became even more wicked. He confused their language so that no one could understand each other. The brother of Jared did not want his language to be confused. He said a prayer.

- *How is saying a prayer a way to exercise faith? (Answer: When we pray to Heavenly Father, we have faith He will hear us even though we cannot see Him.)*

Heavenly Father heard the brother of Jared's prayer. He did not confuse the language of Jared's family or their friends. They could still understand each other. The brother of Jared knew his family needed to leave that wicked place and go somewhere new.

Time to Share

- *When they left, who needed to exercise faith? (Answer: Jared, his brother, and everyone who came with them needed to have faith in Heavenly Father's plan for them.)*

They traveled in the wilderness for a long time. Heavenly Father showed them the way to go.

- *Can you think of any other groups of people who were led through the wilderness by faith? (Answers could include: Lehi's family, the children of Israel, the pioneers, and so on.)*

Finally, they reached the ocean. The brother of Jared did not know how they would cross it, but he knew they could do it with the Lord's help.

- *Have you ever had to do something that seemed impossible? How did your faith help you? (This question could have many correct answers.)*

The Lord told the brother of Jared to build barges to cross the ocean. The barges had to be built a special way so that they would not sink. When the barges were finished, they were so tightly built that air and light couldn't get inside. It seemed like following the Lord's instructions had caused more problems.

- *Does it ever seem like following the Lord's commandments has made life harder than it would've been otherwise? What should you do if this happens? (Answer: We should continue to have faith and keep an eternal perspective.)*

The Lord told the brother of Jared to cut holes in the barges to let air in. But when the brother of Jared asked the Lord what they should do to get light in the barges, the Lord told him to think about it and come up with a solution on his own.

- *Why does the Lord sometimes wait to tell us an answer or prompt us to come up with our own solutions? (Answer: He wants us to learn and study it out in our own minds first.)*

The brother of Jared decided to bring sixteen small, white stones to the Lord. He asked the Lord to touch the stones and make them glow so that the stones would light up the inside of the barges. Jesus agreed. When He touched the stones with His finger, the brother of Jared saw Jesus's finger and was astonished.

- *What did Jesus say was the reason that the brother of Jared could see His finger? See Ether 3:8–9. (Answer: The brother of Jared had "exceeding faith.")*

Because of his faith, the brother of Jared was able to see Jesus's finger and then His whole body. His faith helped the brother of Jared to keep going when things seemed hard and to accomplish many wonderful things, including taking his family and friends across the ocean to a new land of promise.

APPLICATION

Ask the children how they can exercise their faith like the brother of Jared. Have them complete the following sentence: "This week, I will exercise my faith by _____." If time permits, you may want to have them color a picture of several ways to exercise faith (such as praying, fasting, paying tithing, bearing testimony, following a prompting).

REVIEW

Help the children understand that faith is a principle of action. We need to confidently act upon the things that we believe to be true. When we exercise our faith, Heavenly Father will bless us to know that the things we are doing are right. Share with them how this principle has enriched your own life.

Week 2: Repentance Helps Me Return to Heavenly Father

ATTENTION ACTIVITY

Let a few children scribble or draw on the board for a minute, and then have another child come and erase what they've done. Repeat this process a few times until it is time to begin. Explain that you'll be talking about how we can "erase" the mistakes we've made through repentance.

SCRIPTURE

D&C 58:43

TALK

Saul was a wicked man. He did not like the people who followed Christ—the Christians. He tried to hurt them and get them to stop meeting. One day, he was on his way to a place called Damascus to find more Christians and put them in prison. But then, as he was walking, he saw a light and heard Jesus speaking.

Jesus told Saul to stop hurting the Christians. Saul was afraid and fell down. He asked Jesus what he was supposed to do. Jesus told him to go to Damascus, where he would learn more.

When the light went away and Saul got up to go to Damascus, he realized he was blind. His friends helped him get to Damascus, and for three days Saul could not see. He did not eat or drink. Then a man named Ananias came to give Saul a blessing. After the blessing, Saul could see again. He wanted to know more about Jesus, and soon he was baptized.

Saul repented. Instead of hurting the Christians, he helped them spread the word about Jesus. Saul changed his name to Paul and became one of the greatest missionaries of the early Church.

LESSON

Discussion: Explain to the children that while Heavenly Father does not want us to make mistakes, He knows that we will. He still loves us, even when we do something wrong, but He wants us to repent and not make that mistake again. His plan provided a way for us to repent by using the Atonement.

- Why do we need to repent?
- What does it mean to confess and forsake? (See D&C 58:43.)

Even though it is hard and sometimes painful to repent when we do something wrong, repenting always makes us feel better in the end.

ACTIVITY

To reinforce the idea that repentance can help us change ourselves and our lives, ask the children to imagine how certain scripture stories might've ended more happily if some people repented.

- What if the people in Noah's time had repented before the flood?
- What if the pharaoh of Egypt had repented and let the people of Israel go before the Lord told Moses to send the plagues?
- What if Laman and Lemuel had repented and become good after they got the brass plates? How would their family's story and the entire Book of Mormon have changed if that had happened?
- What if the Jews had repented and accepted Christ instead of crucifying Him?
- What if the Nephites had repented and become good again at the end of the Book of Mormon when Mormon was leading them in battle?

Have the children act out or illustrate how one or more of these stories might have ended.

APPLICATION

Teach the children how to repent by having them practice. Have them close their eyes and consider the things they have done wrong or any mistakes they have made in the past few days or weeks. Do not ask them to list their poor choices out loud, but do ask them how they feel about those choices. Tell them that they do not need to feel sad forever. Instead, they can pray and ask God to forgive them. Give them a minute or two to pray silently and ask for forgiveness. Then encourage them to change by trying to make amends to others who have been hurt by their choices and also by not making those wrong choices again.

REVIEW

Help the children to understand that the sooner they repent, the sooner they can start to feel better. Encourage them to repent often so that they can continue on their journeys back to Heavenly Father.

Week 3: The Ordinance of Baptism Lets Me Enter the Gate to God's Kingdom

ATTENTION ACTIVITY

Invite four or five children to come to the front of the room. Have two of them act as a gate by facing each other and stretching out their arms toward one other. Have the other children stand behind the gate and stay there until the gate is opened. For younger children, give them verbal clues to help them guess what the gate is—baptism. For older children, write seven blank spaces on the board and have them guess letters, filling in any they guess correctly. When the children finish, have them, acting as the gate, open their arms so the other children can walk through. Then have all the children return to their seats.

SCRIPTURE

2 Nephi 31:17

TALK

Gemma has made lots of promises in her life. When she was little, she promised her parents she wouldn't cross the street without holding a grown-up's hand. Then she got a little older and she promised that she would be good for her babysitter whenever her parents went out. One time, she promised her little sister, Mia, that if Mia would help Gemma with her chores, Gemma would play dolls with her all day. The girls had fun working on chores together and even more fun playing.

Now Gemma is getting ready to make a very important promise. This time, she will be promising something to the Lord. Gemma is getting ready to be baptized. When we are baptized, we promise Heavenly Father that we will look out for others and try to serve them. We promise to obey the commandments and always remember Jesus.

In return, Heavenly Father promises that we can always have His Spirit with us. This kind of promise is called a covenant. The covenant of baptism is special because it is the first covenant you get to make with Heavenly Father. It is the first step on your journey back to him.

LESSON

Discussion: Explain to the children that the Lord's people have always been baptized to show their commitment to Heavenly Father.

Help the children understand that baptism is symbolic of being born again. When we are baptized, we go all the way down under the water, and when we come out, we are completely clean. We can start fresh and begin our new lives as members of the Church.

- How is being baptized like being washed clean?
- Why do we need to be baptized by immersion?

ACTIVITY

Invite three or four of the children in your ward who were recently baptized to be your panel of experts and share their experiences with the rest of the children. This may mean these children will need to miss part of their lesson, so be sure to ask their teacher if that is okay.

Invite your panel of experts to sit or stand at the front of the room and tell the other children what happened on the day they were baptized. Have them share how they felt that day. Then ask them how their lives have changed since they were baptized.

After they have shared their experiences, invite the other children to ask your experts any questions they may have about being baptized.

APPLICATION

Read Mosiah 18:8–10 together. Review the actions we promise to take when we are baptized.

- Come into the fold of God.
- Be called His people.
- Bear one another's burdens, that they may be light.
- Mourn with those that mourn.
- Comfort those that stand in need of comfort.
- Stand as His witnesses at all times and in all things and places.
- Serve Him and keep His commandments.

For each of these actions, discuss together what the children might do in our day to fulfill these promises. (For example, they could stand as witnesses by asking their friends not to use the Lord's name in vain.)

REVIEW

Share what you remember about your own baptism day. Encourage children who have been baptized to record their thoughts and feelings about their baptism. Bear your testimony of the importance of being baptized and help the children understand how pleased Heavenly Father is when we choose to take that first step back to Him.

Week 4: The Gift of the Holy Ghost Will Help Me Return to Heavenly Father

ATTENTION ACTIVITY

While all of the children are entering the room, talking, and getting ready for Primary, play the song "The Holy Ghost" on your phone, tablet, or on another music player. Play the song at a low volume at first. You may even want to have the pianist play a different song for the prelude at the same time. When the song is over, ask the children how many of them heard it. Ask if they can tell you what the song is about. If they did not hear it, ask them to try again. This time, do not have the pianist play a prelude, but also do not turn up the volume of your music player.

See how many children can hear the song and tell you about its message after the second time you play it. Explain to the children that the Holy Ghost may be hard to hear over the distractions all around us. That's why we need to learn how to focus and pay attention to the Spirit's still, small voice.

SCRIPTURE

D&C 130:22

TALK

Sienna has a special job at home. Each day, she watches for the mail to be delivered. When it arrives, she brings it inside and sorts it into piles for each person in her family. Sienna loves it when she gets mail for herself. It's fun to open up envelopes and see what's inside.

But best of all is when Sienna gets a package. Each year for her birthday, her grandmother sends her a special package with a present inside. Sienna loves to open the package and see what her gift is.

Heavenly Father has given each one of us a gift. This gift did not come in a package; it is the gift of the Holy Ghost. When we are baptized, we can receive this gift, which will help us to return to Him.

The Holy Ghost is a little bit like a mail carrier because He delivers messages to us from Jesus and Heavenly Father. We all need to learn how to listen for the messages that the Holy Ghost wants to deliver to us. That is how we can enjoy the Holy Ghost as our special gift from God.

LESSON

Discussion: Help the children to understand that the Holy Ghost is a wonderful companion for us on our journey back to Heavenly Father. Because He does not have a physical body, He can be with us all the time. Tell them that any time they need to make a choice, the Holy Ghost will guide them to choose what is right. They simply need to learn how to hear and feel His promptings.

- What might distract you from feeling the influence of the Holy Ghost?
- What could you do to eliminate those distractions, especially when you really need an answer?

ACTIVITY

Draw a stick figure on the board. Explain to the children that this figure represents them. For each symbol in the chart below, invite one of the children to come up and draw that symbol in the given location. As you add the symbols to your drawing, ask the children how the Holy Ghost might relate to that symbol. Then discuss the corresponding explanation with them.

Symbol	Explanation
Draw a lightbulb or star near the stick figure's head.	The Holy Ghost can give us good ideas or help us to think more clearly.
Draw a heart on the figure's chest.	The Holy Ghost gives us feelings of peace, love, and happiness.
Draw scriptures on the figure's torso.	The Holy Ghost reminds us to feed our spirits in addition to our bodies.
Draw hands on the figure.	The Holy Ghost can prompt us to be generous and serve others.
Draw feet on the figure.	The Holy Ghost sometimes prompts us to be in a certain place at a certain time in order for something to happen. He will also prompt you to leave a place that is dangerous.

Time to Share

APPLICATION

Emphasize the idea that not everyone feels the Holy Ghost in the same way. Have the children discuss what the Holy Ghost feels like to them. Give the children a challenge to interview someone they know about the Holy Ghost. Have them ask the person to tell them what the Holy Ghost feels like to the interviewee. The children could choose to interview a parent, grandparent, home teacher, or leader.

REVIEW

Encourage the children to pay attention to what the Holy Ghost feels like to them. Share your own experience of a time when you felt the influence of the Holy Ghost. Then share a few ideas that have helped you to focus on the Spirit, even when your life has been extra busy or distracting. These might include taking time away from music and other media or getting up a little earlier to study the scriptures. Conclude with your own testimony of the Holy Ghost as a member of the Godhead and as a powerful gift for us in our lives.

Chapter 7: July
The Temple Is Heavenly Father's House

MULTIMEDIA RESOURCES

"Teachings of Mormon Prophet - Joseph Smith: Temple Ordinances"—YouTube, LDS Church History, 1:44 (https://www.youtube.com/watch?v=ASgX10llA64)

"Temples Are a Beacon"—YouTube, Mormon Channel, 2:50 (https://www.youtube.com/watch?v=73jY8xH_vhc)

"Why Mormons Build Temples"—YouTube, Mormon Channel, 3:14 (https://www.youtube.com/watch?v=-x_-TQivCx8)

"Blessings of the Temple"—YouTube, Mormon Channel, 3:59 (https://www.youtube.com/watch?v=vC40r19cLuw)

"Mormon Temples: The Blessings of Temples"—YouTube, Mormon Channel, 3:32 (https://www.youtube.com/watch?v=XLXYxmaHWQs)

SONG LIST

Focus Song: "I Love to See the Temple" (95)

Additional Songs: "Families Can Be Together Forever" (188), "Truth from Elijah" (90)

Review Songs: "If I Listen with My Heart," "I Will Follow God's Plan," "Stand for the Right," "Praise to the Man"

GOSPEL ART BOOK

"My Father's House" (52)

Week 1: Heavenly Father's People Have Always Built Temples

ATTENTION ACTIVITY

Have the children draw pictures of their dream houses. They may choose to include the people they would want to have living there, what the house would be made of, any special rooms or features, and so on. Give them a few minutes to draw, and then let one or two children come up to the front and tell the others about their houses.

SCRIPTURE

D&C 88:119

TALK

When Lehi told his family that they needed to leave Jerusalem, he explained that Heavenly Father wanted to lead them to a new land. He called this place "the promised land" because Heavenly Father had promised to give it to their family. Heavenly Father also promised that it would be a good land, where they would be richly blessed.

So they left Jerusalem and spent many years traveling in the wilderness. They walked for a long time. When they reached the ocean, they rested there for a while, but they knew they would need to keep going to find the promised land. Nephi built a ship to take them across the ocean. It took the ship a long time to make it to land. Many times, Laman and Lemuel wanted to give up. But Nephi and Lehi helped them to keep going.

Finally, they reached the promised land. They were all so happy to be in their new home. They wanted to thank Heavenly Father for guiding them in their journey. They built many houses and other buildings, but the most important one was the temple. They knew the temple is a place where Jesus and Heavenly Father can come to visit the earth, and where we can feel closer to them.

LESSON

Discussion: Refer to the attention activity and explain that Heavenly Father also has a house here on the earth. In fact, He has several. These houses are near perfect and beautiful, like something you would dream about. They are our temples. Because they are His houses, they must be built according to His instructions and plans. And each of us must follow His commandments in order to enter them.

- Why does a temple need to be perfect, clean, and beautiful?
- What do we need to do to be worthy to enter the temple?

ACTIVITY

Tell the children that today they will all be temple time travelers! Explain that throughout time, God's people have built temples for Him to visit. Divide the children into four groups and assign each group a temple from the list below. Make sure each group includes one or two teachers. You may want to have each group meet in a different corner of the room. Have them read their scripture passage together, talk about their temple, and prepare to share what they know with the other groups.

Temple	Scripture Passage	Important Events or Significance	*Gospel Art Book* Picture
Tabernacle	Exodus 25:1–2, 8–9	Went with the children of Israel in the desert; helped them to prepare to build their permanent temple in Jerusalem.	"Moses Gives Aaron the Priesthood" (15)
Jerusalem Temple in the time of Christ	Matthew 21:12–14; John 8:2	Jesus taught the people there; they came to offer sacrifices, according to the law of Moses.	"Jesus Cleansing the Temple" (51) and "My Father's House" (52)
Nephite temple in Bountiful	3 Nephi 11:1–2, 8–12	Jesus appeared to the Nephites at the temple to teach them the gospel.	"Jesus Teaching in the Western Hemisphere" (82)
Kirtland Temple	D&C 110:1–16	Joseph taught the Saints there; numerous ancient prophets came to restore priesthood keys; and the Savior appeared and accepted the temple.	"Elijah Appearing in the Kirtland Temple" (95) and "The Kirtland Temple" (117)

When the groups are ready to share, have one group at a time come to the front of the room and present their temple. If possible, have

Time to Share

them display their picture from the *Gospel Art Book* and talk about what it depicts. In between groups, have the children pretend to be traveling through time together.

APPLICATION

Encourage the children to share what they have learned about ancient and modern temples with their families. Sing "I Love to See the Temple" (95) together.

REVIEW

Help the children understand that God's people have always built temples. Explain that in some ways our temples have changed over time. For example, the Saints in Kirtland often used the temple for regular Church meetings, whereas now we use them only for special ordinances. However, their basic purpose as a place for God to dwell on earth has remained the same throughout time. Testify of the peace that comes into our lives when we worship at the temple regularly. Tell the children how important is to prepare early to someday enter the temple.

Week 2: My Family Is Blessed through Temple Ordinances

ATTENTION ACTIVITY

Play "Name That Temple." Show the children several pictures of temples from around the world and see if they can guess which temples they are. You can find photos of the temples on the Church's website at https://www.lds.org/church/temples/gallery?lang=eng.

SCRIPTURE

D&C 132:46

TALK

Zachary loves his family. He lives with his parents and sisters, so he sees them every day. He loves his grandparents, aunts, uncles, and cousins too. But some of them live far away. Zachary and his sisters like to talk to them on the phone or online. Zachary also likes to draw pictures and send them to the people in his family. Sometimes, his mom reads emails or posts from his aunts and uncles and grandparents out loud so that Zachary and his dad and sisters can enjoy them.

We are blessed to have many ways to stay connected to our families. With phone calls, emails, video chats, and social media, we can always be close to the people we love, even if they are far away. These tools help us to love our family members more.

Heavenly Father has given us another way to stay connected to our families. It's called the sealing power. This power works not just on earth but also after we die. Even though we can't call or email our family members after they pass away, we can still be connected to them because we are sealed to them and they are sealed to us. Families are sealed together in the temple. When we are sealed in the temple as a family, we can stay connected as a family after we die. This is one of the greatest blessings Heavenly Father has given us.

LESSON

Discussion: (Throughout this lesson, be sensitive to children whose family situations are difficult.) Explain that the most important part of Heavenly Father's plan was for us to come to earth and be part of a family. The family proclamation tells us that families are central to that plan. Temples are the only way to keep our family together after we die.

- Why is it important to be sealed to your family in the temple?
- What can we do to make sure our families stay worthy of temple blessings?

ACTIVITY

Have each child create a family banner. Give each child a piece of paper (a long, legal-sized paper would be ideal, or a regular 8.5 x 11 paper cut in half lengthwise). At the top of their papers, help the children write, "My Family Can Be Forever." Underneath this, have them draw a picture of a temple, and under this have them draw each member of their families. Encourage them to decorate the rest of the banner with symbols of things their families do together.

APPLICATION

Let the children show their banners to their classmates. Point out that everyone's banner looks different, just as every family looks different. Emphasize that it does not matter what our families look like or who they include. The important thing is that we love our family members and we all try to make good choices so that we can be sealed in the temple forever. Encourage the children to share their banners with their families.

REVIEW

Make sure the children understand that Heavenly Father sent us to our families for a reason. He wants us to learn how to love, and families are the best place for us to learn to love and serve. Bear your testimony of eternal families. Share with the children some of the ways you are trying to help your own family become a forever family.

Week 3: The Pioneers Built Temples through Hard Work and Sacrifice

ATTENTION ACTIVITY

Watch "Chapter 59: Endowments Are Performed in the Nauvoo Temple: November 1845 - February 1846"—Mormon Channel, 1:12 (https://www.youtube.com/watch?v=BQhRt9XGCEM).

SCRIPTURE

D&C 124:26–27

TALK

Every day on the way home from school last year, Sadie and Davis walked past the vacant lot in their neighborhood. The lot was full of weeds, garbage, and old broken things. It looked like a big mess. Then one day, their dad announced that they were going to do something about it. On Saturday morning, he woke the whole family up early. Together, they carried garbage bags, rakes, and shovels to the vacant lot.

When they looked at the lot, Sadie and Davis groaned. They were still sleepy and cold. Their mom pulled on some gloves and put trash into the trash bag. She asked Sadie and Davis to help, so they did. After a while, something strange happened. Sadie and Davis started having fun, and the lot started to look nicer. Their dad mowed the overgrown grass, and their neighbor Mrs. Jones stopped by to transplant some of her flowers along the street. By lunchtime, the lot looked great, and the kids were excited to have a new place to play. Even though it had taken a lot of hard work, Sadie and Davis were proud of what they had done. Heavenly Father wants us to learn how to work hard and make sacrifices. He asks us to help Him build His kingdom so that we can learn to be good workers and give up the things that we want now so that Heavenly Father can have the things that He wants—that's because we know that what Heavenly Father really wants is for all of us to be happy forever.

LESSON

Discussion: Refer to the scripture above (D&C 124:26–27). If you did not have a child read it earlier, do so now, or read it aloud yourself. Have the children identify all the things the Lord asked the pioneers to use when they built the temple. Point out that the Saints were not wealthy at that time, and they all had to sacrifice their time and money to build the temple and make it beautiful.

- Why do you think Heavenly Father asked the Saints to make the temple out of expensive materials?
- What can we learn when we're asked to give something up? When we are asked to sacrifice, does it help the person we are sacrificing for or does it help us? Both?

ACTIVITY

Take the children for a "pioneer trek" (walk) around the outside of your church building, weather permitting. Have them pay special attention to the building. When you get back to the Primary room, ask the children if they think it would take a long time to build the church without big construction vehicles. Show the following pictures from the *Gospel Art Book* and explain that when these temples were built, the pioneers who built them had to do all of the work by hand.

- "Kirtland Temple" (117)
- "Nauvoo Temple" (118)
- "Salt Lake City Temple" (119)

You may also wish to show photos of the temples in St. George, Utah; Logan, Utah; and Manti, Utah.

Discuss the difficulties that might've arisen during construction of these temples. Ask the children to think about how they would have responded to the challenge of walking across the plains or working hard building a temple.

APPLICATION

Encourage the children to work hard like the pioneers. Help them think of a job they could do to help in their families; ideally, it should be a chore that they are not already assigned to do. Challenge them to cheerfully do their work all week without forgetting or complaining.

REVIEW

Testify of the importance of hard work and sacrifice. Explain that the pioneers were happy to build the temples, even though it was hard, because they knew how important temple work was. Share your feelings about the temple and your gratitude for the pioneers who left us all a legacy of faith and sacrifice.

Week 4: I Can Go to the Temple If I Prepare and Stay Worthy

ATTENTION ACTIVITY

Follow up on the challenge you gave the children the previous week to work hard like the pioneers. Invite a few children to stand up and share their thoughts and feelings about their experiences. Encourage any children who forgot to try again this week.

SCRIPTURE

Proverbs 20:11

TALK

Last year, something very exciting happened for Brooklyn and her family. They got to go to the temple! Brooklyn is only eleven, so she can't do baptisms for the dead yet. But last year, her family got to attend an open house for a brand new temple. Each person in her family had to have a special reserved ticket to attend. When Brooklyn walked inside the temple, she was amazed at how beautiful everything was. She had never been inside a temple before. She saw the baptistry and felt the Spirit. After the tour was over, Brooklyn took a picture of the temple that she keeps in her room to remind her of that day.

Before a temple is dedicated, anyone can come inside to see it during the open house. The only thing you need is a ticket. But after a temple has been dedicated, you must be worthy to enter. Instead of a ticket, you need a recommend. Temple recommends are given only to those who keep the commandments and have a testimony of Jesus.

Brooklyn knows that she can prepare now to have her own temple recommend one day soon. She can prepare by studying the scriptures, serving others, and trying to always choose the right. And that's how you can prepare too!

LESSON

Discussion: Remind the children about the attention activity and the fact that there were probably a few children who forgot to complete the challenge to work hard like a pioneer. (Use generalizations to avoid calling out those who did not complete the assignment.) Explain that when we came to the earth, Heavenly Father knew we might forget to serve Him sometimes. He designed special covenants and ordinances to help us remember our promise to choose the right.

- Have you made any covenants already? What did you promise to do?

Explain that in the temple we make more covenants and participate in sacred ordinances. Once we have done these things for ourselves, we can return often to the temple to do this work for the dead. Returning to repeat these things helps us remember the covenants we have made. Tell the children that when they turn twelve, they can attend the temple to be baptized for the dead, just as they were (or will be) baptized for themselves first.

ACTIVITY

Help the children to prepare for temple service by reviewing "My Gospel Standards," available online at https://www.lds.org/media-library/images/my-gospel-standards-183289?lang=eng.

Assign each class two or three sentences from "My Gospel Standards." You may want to print out slips of paper with these assignments for the teachers. Have the classes take a few minutes to discuss their sections, and then think of a symbolic action or actions for those sentences. Have each class share their action(s) with the rest of the group. When you have finished, read through the entire document and have the children perform the actions for each sentence or group of sentences as you read them.

APPLICATION

Encourage the children to choose one of the commitments in "My Gospel Standards" to improve on. Remind them that they can practice keeping their commitments and promises now so they will be ready to make sacred covenants in the temple one day.

REVIEW

Express to the children how beautiful and clean the temple is. Explain that part of the reason the temple is so special is that each person who enters is worthy and trying to obey Heavenly Father. Encourage them to prepare now and stay worthy so that they can enter the temple themselves and participate in the sacred work there.

Chapter 8: August
My Body Is a Temple

MULTIMEDIA RESOURCES

"Chapter 31: The Word of Wisdom (February 1833)"—YouTube, LDS Media Library, 2:10 (https://www.lds.org/media-library/video/2010-06-32- chapter-31-the-word-of-wisdom-february-1833?lang=eng)

"A Mormon Olympian"—YouTube, Mormon Channel, 5:39 (https://www.youtube.com/watch?v=5IOYmJMzyEg)

"195 Dresses"—YouTube, LDS Youth, 5:11 (https://www.youtube.com/watch?v=q1IbEuq2gf8)

"Dayton's Legs"—YouTube, LDS Youth, 3:02 (https://www.youtube.com/watch?v=bwwxBjpvDVQ)

SONG LIST

Focus Song: "The Lord Gave Me a Temple" (153)

Additional Songs: "The Word of Wisdom" (154), "I'm Trying to Be like Jesus" (78)

Review Songs: "If I Listen with My Heart," "I Will Follow God's Plan," "Stand for the Right," "Praise to the Man," "I Love to See the Temple"

GOSPEL ART BOOK

"Salt Lake Temple" (119)

Week 1: I Will Take Care of My Body Because It Is a Temple

ATTENTION ACTIVITY

Sing "Head, Shoulders, Knees, and Toes" with the actions (275). Then sing both verses of "My Heavenly Father Loves Me" (288).

SCRIPTURE

1 Corinthians 3:16

TALK

Connor and Wyatt love to be outside. They go to the park and run around on the playground. They play sports with their dad and help their mom take care of the backyard. But they couldn't do any of these things without their bodies.

Our bodies are a special gift from God to help us enjoy this world He has made. With our bodies, we can see and taste and feel things that we couldn't experience otherwise. They let us run around and play. They do amazing things to help us get better when we feel sick. They work hard so we can do all the things we want to get done.

That is why we need to take good care of our bodies. Jesus has told us how to care for our bodies. He has commanded us to eat healthy foods and stay away from those foods and other things that are bad for us. He wants us to enjoy our bodies by being active and getting enough sleep. We should try to take care of our bodies because they are our temples. Taking care of our bodies shows Heavenly Father we are grateful for them and for the world He made us for us.

LESSON

Discussion: Explain to the children that our bodies are like temples. Have them think about the temple and what a beautiful, clean, and holy place it is. Only good things can go inside the temple, and we use temples to perform sacred work for our Heavenly Father. Our bodies are the same. We need to keep them clean. We need to put only good foods inside them, and we must make sure we use them to work hard and do good things. We also need to let our bodies rest when they are tired, just like our temples close each night and on Sundays.

- What could you do to care for your body?
- Why is it important to treat our bodies well?

ACTIVITY

Help the children appreciate how beautiful and unique each person's body is by having each child stand and complete the sentence, "My favorite thing about my body is _____." Encourage them to think about what their bodies can do, rather than simply what they look like. Be sensitive about comparing bodies and help the children to think of their bodies positively.

APPLICATION

Tell the children that their challenge this week is to try experiencing something new with their bodies. They may want to try playing a new sport, tasting a new food, visiting a new museum, or listening to some new and uplifting music. After they have tried the new thing, encourage them to thank Heavenly Father for their bodies.

REVIEW

Explain to the children that one of the reasons we were so excited to come to the earth was to gain a body. Heavenly Father gave us bodies so that we could learn to become more like Him. We need to make good choices and care for our bodies. Bear your testimony of the joy you have experienced from having a body and share how this helps you experience life on earth more fully.

Week 2: I Will Dress Modestly

ATTENTION ACTIVITY

As they come in the room, hand each child a small piece of paper with a stick figure on it. You may draw each one by hand or make copies. Invite the children to draw modest clothing on their stick figures.

SCRIPTURE

1 Corinthians 6:20

TALK

Mariah is a great dancer. She loves to go to dance class and practice new routines. She also loves performing in recitals for all her friends and family. One time, just before a big recital, Mariah came to class and saw the new costume she would be wearing in the recital. The costume was pretty, but it was not modest. Mariah felt worried. She wanted to dance in the recital, but she knew it was important to be modest.

After class, she told her mom about the costume. Her mom told her not to worry. She was sure they could work something out. The next week, Mariah's mom came to class with her and asked if they could take the costume home and make a few changes to it. Mariah's teacher agreed. Mariah helped her mom with the sewing, and soon they had a costume that was even more beautiful than before and modest.

Mariah was happy she had a costume she could wear without being worried. And everyone was happy when they watched Mariah dancing beautifully in the big recital. Heavenly Father has asked us to be modest and show respect for our bodies. He will bless us when we make good choices about what to wear to church, school, or anywhere we're going.

LESSON

Discussion: Explain that Heavenly Father has asked us to dress modestly. He has promised that when we do so, we will feel good about our bodies and be able to do all of the fun things we like to do without worrying about our clothing.

ACTIVITY

Use the following game to have a discussion with the children about modesty. Bring ten articles of miscellaneous clothing with you, such as a large shirt, gloves, a watch, a belt, a scarf, a hat, boots, and sunglasses.

Invite a volunteer to come to the front of the room. Explain to the children that the object of this game is to get all of the clothes onto the child at the front. To do this, they will need to answer questions correctly. Each time they answer the questions below, have the child at the front put on another piece of clothing.

Note: for younger children, you may want to use only the first five questions and have the child in front put on two articles of clothing for each correct answer.

Question	Answer
Who has commanded us to dress modestly?	God has revealed this commandment to our modern prophets.
How does dressing modestly help us be more comfortable?	We don't need to worry about what we look like or what might show. We can just enjoy whatever activity we're doing.
Who can we ask if we are not sure if something is modest or not?	Parents, teachers, or friends who have also committed to being modest.
What should you do if you feel uncomfortable wearing something?	Listen to the Holy Ghost. He is likely prompting you to go find something more modest to wear.
How can we help others to understand why it is that we dress modestly?	We could explain that being modest helps us to respect our bodies and be happy.
Besides our clothes, what else is part of a modest appearance?	The way we dress is only one part of a modest appearance. We should also make sure that we keep our bodies clean and our hair nice and well done.
Why is it important not to draw too much attention to our bodies?	When we draw too much attention to our bodies, we may distract others from our spirits and personalities. They may think of us only as what we look like instead of who we really are inside.

Time to Share

Question	Answer
Does Heavenly Father judge us by how fancy our clothes are?	Of course not. He judges us by our thoughts and our hearts. Have one of the children read 1 Samuel 16:7.
What does it mean to "let virtue garnish thy thoughts"? (See D&C 121:45)	Having virtuous thoughts means that we think about good things—not about things that would make the Holy Ghost want to leave us.
What are some resources that could help you to learn more about modesty and virtue?	You could find more information in the *For the Strength of Youth* pamphlet; on the Church's website; in conference talks; or by talking to parents, teachers, and leaders.

APPLICATION

Have the children think about the clothes they are going to wear the next day. Encourage them to pick out a modest outfit for the next day as soon as they return home. Ask them to commit to dressing modestly throughout their lives.

REVIEW

Tell the children that Heavenly Father is pleased when we dress modestly. He wants us to enjoy wearing clothing that fits well and helps us to be happy. The Holy Ghost will help us to know what we should wear. He will also help us to keep our thoughts and actions pure and virtuous. Share your testimony of this principle and how it has helped you to be happy.

Week 3: I Will Choose the Right Foods

ATTENTION ACTIVITY

Tell the children you are going to name several different foods and that they should stand up when they hear a food they like and sit down when they hear a food they do not like. Make sure to name a variety of healthy foods (such as apples, cucumbers, tomatoes, chicken, and spaghetti), a few things that are not as healthy (such as chips and ice cream), and one or two that are against the Word of Wisdom (such as coffee).

SCRIPTURE

D&C 89:18–20

TALK

James is a picky eater. His parents tell him he should try more foods, but he only likes macaroni and cheese, cereal, and jam sandwiches. His brother Owen isn't picky at all—he'll eat almost anything. Even things like broccoli, fish, and some fried bugs their dad brought back from one of his business trips. James and his mom thought the bugs looked gross. They couldn't believe Owen and Dad ate them.

When Heavenly Father created the world, He made lots of different things for us to eat. He wants us to enjoy eating the right things in the right amounts. He revealed a special commandment to Joseph Smith that helps us to know what kinds of food are good for us. This commandment is called the Word of Wisdom. It tells us which foods will help us be healthy and which foods could make us sick.

Following the Word of Wisdom will make our bodies feel good and give us the energy we need to do all the things we enjoy. We should thank Heavenly Father for the Word of Wisdom and do our best to obey it every day.

LESSON

Discussion: Explain that Heavenly Father desires for us to enjoy the bodies He has given us. To make sure our bodies stay healthy and strong, He has given us the Word of Wisdom. Review the basic principles of the Word of Wisdom, as outlined in Doctrine and Covenants 89.

- What foods should we not eat? What foods are good for us?

- What promises does Heavenly Father give us if we keep this commandment?

ACTIVITY

Have a few children come to the front of the room and act out the story of Daniel refusing the king's food while you or an older child read the following paraphrased account of Daniel 1.

Nebuchadnezzar was the king of Babylon. He came to Jerusalem and fought the people there. When Nebuchadnezzar won the battle, he took some of the best treasures in Jerusalem back to Babylon with him. He also took some of the best children back to Babylon. Daniel was one of these children. He had three friends who came with him. When Daniel and his friends got to Babylon, Nebuchadnezzar told all of them he would give them rich food and his best wine to drink for three years.

Most of the others were excited about this food. But Daniel and his friends knew that Heavenly Father did not want them to eat the king's food. They asked the men who brought the food in to let them have plain, healthy food instead. The men who brought the food thought that the plain food would make Daniel and his friends sick. The men did not want to get in trouble with King Nebuchadnezzar for switching the food, but Daniel asked them to try it for ten days, and they agreed.

At the end of ten days, Daniel and his friends looked much healthier than everyone else, so the men who brought the food agreed to let them keep eating their healthy food. Heavenly Father blessed Daniel and his friends and made them smarter than the other children.

After the three years were over, all of the children went to meet Nebuchadnezzar again. The king talked to all of the children, but he soon discovered that Daniel and his three friends were the smartest ones. They were even smarter than the king's magicians and astrologers. Heavenly Father had blessed them with wisdom because they obeyed him.

APPLICATION

Have the children draw pictures of healthy foods and encourage them to share these pictures with their families.

REVIEW

Emphasize the importance of caring for our bodies by eating healthy foods. Make sure they understand that great blessings can come to us when we eat the right things and avoid foods that are addictive or bad for us. Share your own feelings about the Word of Wisdom and recommit to making good choices about what you eat.

Week 4: I Will Choose the Right Media

ATTENTION ACTIVITY

Emphasize the power of good media to bring the Spirit by watching one of your favorite Mormon Messages or Church-sponsored YouTube videos. You might consider "The Old Shoemaker," 3:27 (https://www.youtube.com/watch?v=pifDZ1hu6gY), or show "A Mother's Hope: Overcoming Fear through Faith & Hope in God," 3:05 (https://www.youtube.com/watch?v=9ssHhzi7aII).

SCRIPTURE

Article of Faith 1:13

TALK

One time, Landon and Lexi were playing video games at a friend's house. Their friend told them they needed to try a new game that was really cool. But after a few minutes of playing the game, Landon and Lexi looked at each other. They knew this game was not cool. In fact, it was making them feel bad inside. Their mom would not have let them play a game like this, and, more important, the Holy Ghost couldn't be with them if they were playing it.

Landon asked their friend if they could play a different game instead. Lexi suggested one that she knew was good. Their friend agreed, and they had a great time together.

When we see or hear things we know are not good, it can make us feel bad inside. We need to learn how to listen to those feelings and get rid of anything in our lives that would keep the Holy Ghost away. When we have the Holy Ghost with us, we can feel happy and confident. We can know that Heavenly Father is pleased with our choices and feel His love all around us.

LESSON

Discussion: Explain to the children that Heavenly Father has always inspired people to create beautiful, uplifting things for us to enjoy. But some people create things that bring us down or make us feel yucky. We need to learn to use the Holy Ghost to help us choose good media and avoid things that are bad.

- What does the word *media* include? Have the children help you make a list on the board (answers could include books, videos, shows, movies, music, artwork, websites, games, apps, and so on).
- How can we know if something we are watching, reading, or playing is bad for us?

ACTIVITY

Help the children to understand that just as we need to keep our bodies clean and eat healthy food, we also need to make sure our minds stay clean and are filled with good things. Place a glass jar or bowl on the table. Explain that the jar represents our minds, and that we need to fill it with good things so that there's no room for bad things. You may want to draw a face on the jar or bowl.

Hand out small pieces of paper to the children and instruct them to write down the names of their favorite pieces of uplifting media. Refer them to the list on the board for more ideas. For younger children, have them draw a picture or have their teachers write for them. Invite the children to come up one class at a time, tell everyone what they wrote down, and then put their papers into the bowl or jar.

APPLICATION

Have the children work in pairs or small groups to roleplay together and practice choosing good media. Use one or two of the following scenarios or come up with your own, based on the ages and needs of your children.

First scenario: You are listening to the radio in the car with your whole family. A bad song starts playing, but your parents don't notice because they are busy driving and talking. What do you do?

Second scenario: Your teacher wants to show a movie in class tomorrow that you know includes bad scenes. All of your friends are excited to watch the movie in class. What do you do?

Third scenario: You borrow your mom's tablet to look something up online. An ad comes up that shows inappropriate images. What do you do?

Fourth scenario: You and your brother had a fun time smashing monsters in your new game, but after you finish playing, you realize you feel angry and frustrated. What do you do?

Time to Share

Fifth scenario: Your friend lets you borrow her new book. As you're reading, you notice some bad words and realize that the story is very intense. When your mom asks what you're reading, you lie and tell her it's a different book because you're afraid she might not let you read it. What do you do now?

REVIEW

Explain that there is danger in ignoring the Holy Ghost when He tells us something is not appropriate. After a while, the Holy Ghost will stop trying to help us, and we will not be able to tell what is and isn't appropriate. Encourage the children to pray to have the Holy Ghost with them and to follow His promptings so they can keep their minds clean. Bear your testimony of this principle and share any personal experiences you have with trying to keep your own mind clean.

Chapter 9: September
The Gospel Is for Everyone

MULTIMEDIA RESOURCES

"A Day in the Life of a Mormon Missionary at the MTC"—YouTube, Mormon Newsroom, 4:09 (https://www.youtube.com/watch?v=PpEhE_scrs4)

"The Value of a Full-time Mormon Mission"—YouTube, Mormon Channel, 5:22 (https://www.youtube.com/watch?v=3aKU2rkvFQU)

"Mormon Missionaries: An Introduction"—YouTube, Mormon Channel, 2:27 (https://www.youtube.com/watch?v=YGnpHLS81lY)

"I'll Go Where You Want Me to Go"—LDS Media Library, 5:45 (https://www.lds.org/media-library/video/2013-06-1031-ill-go-where-you-want-me-to-go?lang=eng)

SONG LIST

Focus Song: "A Child's Prayer" (12)

Additional Songs: "I Want to Be a Missionary Now" (168), "I Hope They Call Me on a Mission" (169), "We'll Bring the World His Truth" (172)

Review Songs: "If I Listen with My Heart," "I Will Follow God's Plan," "Stand for the Right," "Praise to the Man," "I Love to See the Temple," "The Lord Gave Me a Temple"

GOSPEL ART BOOK

"Go Ye Therefore" (61)

Week 1: The Scriptures Say That Jesus Wants Everyone to Know the Truth

ATTENTION ACTIVITY

Bring a stack of papers and ask one child to pass the papers out one at a time to each person in the room. Then collect all the papers again and have one child from each class come up and pass out papers to the people in their class. Ask the children if it was faster to pass out the papers individually or to have several people working together. Explain that when we all help spread the gospel, we can make sure that the message of the restored gospel spreads more quickly to those who want to know the truth.

SCRIPTURE

D&C 4:3–4

TALK

When Jesus was on the earth, He preached the gospel to His Apostles and disciples in Jerusalem and the area near there. After He died, the Apostles kept teaching these same people, who were known as Jews.

Then one night, Peter had a dream. In his dream, Peter was told three times to eat food that was forbidden by the law of Moses. Peter thought this was wrong. When he woke up, he kept thinking about the dream. Then some men came to see him. The men were not Jews. Heavenly Father helped Peter understand that his dream meant it was time for the gospel to be preached to everyone, not just the Jews. So Peter went with the men and began teaching them about Jesus.

We are blessed to have the fulness of the gospel on the earth. Just like Peter was told to teach everyone, we have been commanded to share the gospel too. This is why we send missionaries all over the world, so that everyone can know the truth and be happy.

LESSON

Discussion: Explain that Heavenly Father created His plan for all of His children. He wants all of us to return and live with Him again. Once we know about Heavenly Father's plan, we need to share what we know with others so that they can return to Heavenly Father too.

- Why does the gospel need to go to everyone?
- What tools do we have today to help us spread the gospel?

ACTIVITY

Help the children see that the Lord has called missionaries in all ages. Display the *Gospel Art Book* pictures listed below on the board and give each class one or two of the scripture clues below. Have them read their scriptures as a class, identify which missionary the scriptures are talking about, and review the story of this missionary together. When they finish, invite one person from each class to come up, take the picture of their missionary off the board, and hold up the picture as they tell the rest of the children about their missionary.

Missionary	Scripture Clue	*Gospel Art Book* Picture
Noah	Moses 8:19–20	"Building the Ark" (7)
Elijah	1 Kings 18:36–39	"Elijah Contends with the Priests of Baal" (20)
Jonah	Jonah 1; 2; 3:1–5	"Jonah" (27)
Stephen	Acts 6:5–8	"Stephen Sees Jesus on the Right Hand of God" (63)
Lehi	1 Nephi 1:18–20	"Lehi Prophesying to the People of Jerusalem" (67)
Abinadi	Mosiah 11:20	"Abinadi before King Noah" (75)
Ammon	Alma 17:16–18	"Ammon Defends the Flocks of King Lamoni" (78)
Samuel	Helaman 13:2–4	"Samuel the Lamanite on the Wall" (81)
Dan Jones (and other latter-day missionaries)	D&C 52:9–11	"Dan Jones Preaching the Gospel in Wales" (100)

APPLICATION

Bring one large piece of paper for each missionary serving from your ward. If you do not have any missionaries currently serving from your ward, bring papers for each missionary serving in your ward. On each paper, write, "Thank you for sharing the gospel, Elder _____ (or

Time to Share

Sister _____)." Invite the children to decorate the papers with pictures or encouraging notes. After the lesson, give these papers to the family of each missionary or to the missionaries themselves.

REVIEW

Bear your testimony of the importance of missionary work. If you served a full-time mission, tell the children where you served and how you feel about the people you served. If you did not serve a mission, tell them about a family member or friend of yours who served.

Week 2: Being a Missionary Blesses Everyone

ATTENTION ACTIVITY

Bring a small jar or bag filled with beans, stones, or marbles. Invite a few children to the front of the room. Tell them that they can each take a bean (or stone or marble), and they can either keep it or they can give it to someone else. However, any time they give theirs away, they can take two more to replace it. When the beans (or stones or marbles) run out, point out that those who shared the most have the most in the end. Explain that this is what it's like to share the blessings of the gospel with others. When we do so, Heavenly Father gives us even more blessings.

SCRIPTURE

2 Nephi 26:13

TALK

When Josh's older sister left on a mission, Josh liked writing her emails and sending her packages, but he was sad because he missed playing with her. For a long time, he wished he could do something to help his sister with her missionary work. Then one day, he read something in one of her emails. His sister said it was much easier to teach people when the people they were teaching already knew someone in the Church. His sister said this was called a referral because someone who was already a member referred the missionaries to someone they could teach.

Josh was excited. Now he knew how to help his sister. He could help her by helping the missionaries in his own ward. All he needed to do was find them someone to teach. Josh prayed for help finding someone. A few days later at school, he ran into one of his friends from his class the year before. Josh remembered how this friend had asked him some questions about the Church.

The Holy Ghost helped Josh to know that this friend was the right person to refer to the missionaries. Now Josh's friend is taking lessons from the missionaries, and Josh gets to come to every one. Josh loves being a missionary, just like his older sister.

Time to Share

LESSON

Discussion: Encourage the children to share the gospel and support missionary work. Help them to understand that missionary work blesses the lives of those who share, those who hear the word, and anyone else involved.

- Who is blessed when we share the gospel?
- How is each person blessed?

ACTIVITY

Watch the video "Your Day for a Mission"—YouTube, LDS Youth, 3:31 (https://www.youtube.com/watch?v=w7qWWLg220Y), and then discuss with the children who was blessed by Sid Going's missionary service.

Then view the video "The Influence of Missionary Work"—YouTube, Mormon Newsroom, 4:12 (https://www.youtube.com/watch?v=FM9_kTF0T9A). Ask the children who was blessed by Junior Reyes's missionary work.

APPLICATION

Explain that it can be easier to share the gospel if you have a plan. Have the children write or draw pictures of their plans to bless others through missionary work. Encourage them to be specific and to think about who they can invite to hear the gospel or attend an upcoming meeting or activity.

REVIEW

Conclude by sharing how you have been blessed by the missionary work of others. Testify of the joy that comes from sharing the gospel.

Week 3: I Want to Serve a Mission One Day

ATTENTION ACTIVITY

Have the pianist play a few notes from some songs about missionary prep (see list below). Invite the children to guess the song after the first few notes. If they can't, play more. After two or three songs, have them guess what the songs are talking about in order to guess the day's topic: preparing to serve a mission. If they don't guess it, play a couple more.

- "I Hope They Call Me on a Mission" (169)
- "We'll Bring the World His Truth" (172)
- "Called to Serve" (174)
- "I Love to See the Temple" (95)
- "Seek the Lord Early" (108)
- "Keep the Commandments" (146)

SCRIPTURE

Helaman 5:12

TALK

Tymber loves going camping with her family. Whenever they go, they always need to pack lots of supplies. Tymber knows that going on a mission takes a lot of preparation too. When she goes camping, she needs a flashlight. This light is like the light that the Holy Ghost gives us to help us see things clearly and understand.

We need the Holy Ghost to prepare for a mission. Tymber also helps her family by remembering their map or GPS. When we prepare for a mission, our map is what we know about Heavenly Father's plan. It tells us where we were before we were born, where we are now, and where we will go after we die. Tymber knows camping requires a tent for shelter if it rains. A tent is like the covenants we make when we are baptized. You need your baptismal covenants and other covenants because they will protect you from danger and temptation when you serve a mission.

Finally, whenever her family goes camping, Tymber loves helping her parents pack lots of yummy food. When we serve missions, our spirits and bodies need lots of food every day. Food for our spirits comes from the scriptures, so we need to make sure we study them before we serve. If we prepare, camping is fun. The same thing is true about a mission. If you prepare now, a mission can be one of the best parts of your life.

Time to Share

LESSON

Discussion: Refer to the attention activity, if you used it. Explain to the children that they knew those songs and could guess them because they had prepared before class without even knowing it. Through other Primary lessons, family home evenings, and their own personal study, they have already begun building a solid foundation in the gospel. If you did not use the scripture above, read it to the children now. Explain that Jesus is our foundation. If the children build upon the things they already know about Him, they will be better prepared to serve missions and share what they know about Jesus with others around the world.

- What does it mean to have a strong gospel foundation?
- What kinds of activities build or hurt your gospel foundation?

ACTIVITY

Invite the missionaries who are serving in your ward or a couple of recently returned missionaries to come to Primary for a Q&A session. Have them each begin by telling the story of how they knew they wanted to serve a mission. Then let the children ask them questions about how they prepared to serve. Examples:

- How did you study the scriptures before you left on your mission?
- Did you save money specifically for your mission?
- Did you learn to cook, do laundry, and clean up?
- What else do you wish you had done to prepare?

APPLICATION

Encourage the children to begin saving for a mission by helping them to set a savings goal for the next few months (perhaps till Christmas or the end of the year). They may want to set a dollar amount or a percentage of whatever they can earn. Help them write down their goals on pieces of paper that they can take home to display. If time permits, they may wish to draw a picture of themselves as missionaries on their papers.

REVIEW

Help the children understand that they can begin preparing now to serve the Lord on full-time missions. Explain that He expects all worthy young men to serve and that young women make invaluable contributions when they serve. Encourage them to do all they can to prepare now so they will be ready when they are old enough to serve.

Week 4: I Want to Be a Missionary Now

ATTENTION ACTIVITY

Play a recording of "The Things I Do" (170) and invite the children to sing along if they know the words. The song is available on lds.org at https://www.lds.org/music/library/childrens-songbook/the-things-i -do?lang=eng.

SCRIPTURE

1 Timothy 4:12

TALK

Aubrey's family is always telling her she's too little to do things. When they went to the fair, Aubrey was too little to ride on the bumper cars. And when it was time for school, Aubrey was too young to go on the bus. She had to stay home with Mom and go to preschool instead. She can't read yet, and she definitely can't help with big chores like mowing the lawn.

But there is one thing Aubrey is not too little to do. Even though she is young, Aubrey can be a missionary. Everyone can be a missionary. It's not hard to do. You just have to live the gospel, be a good example, and tell others about how knowing the truth makes you happy.

Aubrey has been a good missionary to her friend Amanda, who lives across the street. When they play together, Aubrey tries to make sure Amanda has fun. She shares her toys and shows respect. Amanda's mom likes to have Aubrey come over to play because the two girls get along well and are kind to each other. Sometimes being kind is the best way to be a missionary.

No matter how old or young you are, you can be a missionary to the people around you. You can share the gospel through your words and actions. If you try to be good, others will notice and they will want to be good also. That is what Jesus meant when He told us to let our lights shine.

LESSON

Discussion: Explain to the children that missionary work is not just something for full-time missionaries to do. All of us can be missionaries now. Share an experience you had sharing the gospel. Ask the children the following questions and list their answers on the board.

Time to Share

- Who could you share the gospel with?
- What kinds of things could you do to be a missionary now?

ACTIVITY

Play missionary tag by having one child stand up and complete the following sentence: "I could be a missionary to _____ by _____." Fill in the first blank with the name of one of the other children to "tag" him or her and the second blank with a missionary action, such as the ones you have listed on the board. (Example: "I could be a missionary to Tyler by telling him one of my favorite scripture stories.") The child whose name was called is now it. This child should immediately stand up and complete the sentence with a different name and action. Complete this process as quickly as possible until every child has had an opportunity to participate.

Note: You could make this game go faster by splitting the group in two and having the two groups race against each other. However, keep in mind that reverence and learning are more important than speed and competition.

APPLICATION

Obtain pass-along cards for each child and encourage them all to share one with someone they know. The missionaries or your bishop or branch president should be able to order these for you, or they may already have enough on hand for you to use.

REVIEW

Express to the children the joy that comes from sharing the gospel. Read D&C 18:15 and encourage them to seek after the joy of missionary work while they are young.

Chapter 10: October
I Can Talk to God in Prayer

MULTIMEDIA RESOURCES

"Prayer"—YouTube, Mormon Channel, 4:12 (https://www.youtube.com/watch?v=zndsJTdGwLQ)

"President Monson Talks about Prayer"—YouTube, Mormon Channel, 3:44 (https://www.youtube.com/watch?v=iB1SBdmy3JM)

"I Pray When . . . #didyouthinktopray"—YouTube, Mormon Channel, 1:56 (https://www.youtube.com/watch?v=f-5XfAcVvwQ). This may not work well for younger children as it mainly involves reading.

"A Child's Prayer - Mormon Tabernacle Choir"—YouTube, Mormon Tabernacle Choir, 4:09 (https://www.youtube.com/watch?v=bse5TtEuaGk)

SONG LIST

Focus Song: "A Child's Prayer" (12)

Additional Songs: "We Bow Our Heads" (25), "I Pray in Faith" (14), "Love Is Spoken Here" (190)

Review Songs: "If I Listen with My Heart," "I Will Follow God's Plan," "Stand for the Right," "Praise to the Man," "I Love to See the Temple," "The Lord Gave Me a Temple"

GOSPEL ART BOOK

"Young Boy Praying" (111)

Week 1: I Can Pray and Talk to God

ATTENTION ACTIVITY

Divide the board or a large piece of paper into four quadrants and label the quadrants "parents," "teachers," "friends," and "neighbors." Have the children come up and write or draw something in each quadrant that they would talk to those people about. (Example: one child might draw a test or a homework assignment in the section for teachers.) When each quadrant has a few things in it, have the children return to their seats. Then explain that there is one person we can talk to about everything they have put on the board or paper: our Heavenly Father. He cares about every part of our lives because He loves us. He wants us to talk to Him about everything.

SCRIPTURE

2 Nephi 32:8

TALK

Five years after Samuel the Lamanite prophesied about the Savior's birth, many of the Nephites had become wicked. They believed that the time had already passed and the sign Samuel had told them about—that there would be a day and a night and a day without darkness—hadn't happened. The wicked Nephites made fun of those who still believed.

The Nephite believers became sad. Some wondered if they had been wrong to believe in Jesus. They kept hoping that the sign would come soon. The wicked Nephites became more angry. They decided that if the sign didn't come by a certain day, they would kill all the believers on that day. Nephi, the prophet, was sad that the people were so angry and wicked. He did not want the believers to be killed.

Nephi knew he needed to pray. He prayed all day that the sign would come and that those who still believed wouldn't be killed. After a long time, Nephi heard Jesus answer his prayer. Jesus told Nephi that the sign was coming that same night. The next day, Jesus would be born in Jerusalem!

Nephi was so grateful that his prayer had been answered. That night, he and the other believers watched as the sun went down but everything stayed light. They all knew that Jesus had come to the earth to save them, and they rejoiced together.

LESSON

Discussion: Explain that praying is our way to stay connected to Heavenly Father. He loves us, just like our earthly parents do. Before we came to earth, we spent a long time with Heavenly Father. We loved Him, and He taught us many things. Now that we are here on earth, He still loves us and wants to know how we are doing every day.

- Why is it important to pray often?
- How does praying help you to feel Heavenly Father's love and show Him that you love Him too?

ACTIVITY

Bring a long string and invite two children to help you hold it. Have one child stand at the front of the room and hold one end. Have the other child stand at the back of the room and hold the other end. Explain to the other children that the child at the front represents Heavenly Father and the child at the back represents all of us. The string represents prayer because it keeps us connected to Heavenly Father, even when we are far away from Him. Point out that no matter where the child at the back goes, he or she can stay connected to Heavenly Father by the string.

Read D&C 88:63 together. Ask the children to name some ways they have tried to draw nearer to Heavenly Father. Whenever a child gives a good answer, have the child at the back of the room take a step forward. Keep the string taut by gathering it at each end. Continue discussing ways to draw closer to Heavenly Father until all the string is gathered and the two children are standing next to each other.

APPLICATION

Help the children understand that they can pray about anything. Have them form small groups of three or four and discuss what kinds of things they like to talk to Heavenly Father about when they pray.

REVIEW

Encourage the children to pray every day this week by themselves and with their families. Tell them about how you learned to make personal prayer a habit. Share your testimony that Heavenly Father wants to communicate with each of them. He is never too busy to hear and answer the prayers of His children.

Week 2: The Scriptures Teach Us How to Pray

ATTENTION ACTIVITY

Watch "Sermon on the Mount: The Lord's Prayer"—YouTube, Mormon Channel, 2:17 (https://www.youtube.com/watch?v=YzmbL WIqUBk).

SCRIPTURE

Alma 37:37

TALK

Edison and Malvin love their baby sister, Henrietta. They want to help her. Since she is too young to say prayers by herself, the boys pray for her. Edison and Malvin learned how to pray through practice and reading the scriptures.

The scriptures are filled with stories of people who prayed. Moses prayed on Mount Sinai, and God gave him the Ten Commandments. Jesus prayed with His disciples and taught them how to pray the right way. Mormon and Moroni prayed that Heavenly Father would protect the gold plates. Joseph Smith prayed to know the truth. Heavenly Father heard all these prayers. He hears us every time we pray.

Someday Edison and Malvin want to tell Henrietta all about the scripture stories they know. When she is older, they will help her learn to pray like them. They know Heavenly Father will hear her prayers and answer them, just like He hears and and answers their prayers.

LESSON

Discussion: Refer to the video you watched as the attention activity, or summarize Matthew 6:9–13 in your own words. Tell the children that Jesus also taught the Nephites how to pray when He visited them (see 3 Nephi 13). Explain that some people believe in saying the same prayers over and over again.

- Why are we not supposed to repeat the same prayers over and over again?
- What four parts should we include in our prayers? (Invocation to Heavenly Father, expressions of gratitude for our blessings, petitions for things we need, and closing in the name of Jesus Christ.)

ACTIVITY

Have the children act out the story of the Zoramites, who said the same prayer each week on the Rameumptom. You may want to bring a stepstool to represent the Rameumptom. Invite some children to be Zoramites and stand in line to pretend to pray. Ask the other children to be the Nephite missionaries who came to watch the Zoramites, and then taught them the correct way to pray. You may want to have one of the older children or a teacher pretend to be Alma and lead the missionaries in their discussion.

APPLICATION

Help the children to create prayer badges that will remind them to pray throughout the week. Cut out a small circle of paper for each child. Help them write the word *pray* on one side. Then have them color a picture of themselves praying on the other side. Tell them to put the badge on their pillow so they will remember to pray that night. Encourage them to keep the badge in a place where they will see it all week to help them remember to say their personal prayers.

Note: Older children may prefer smaller badges, but younger children may have a harder time drawing in a small area. Consider bringing several sizes of pre-cut circles and letting the children choose which size they want to use. Alternatively, you may choose to cut out the badges as part of the lesson.

REVIEW

Share with the children your favorite scripture story about prayer. Encourage them to pray sincerely and talk with Heavenly Father every day. Point out that the scriptures tell us that prayer will keep us safe from temptation and help us stay close to the Spirit.

Week 3: Heavenly Father Hears My Prayers

ATTENTION ACTIVITY

Have one child stand in a far corner of the room and whisper the sentence, "Heavenly Father hears my prayers." Tell the children to raise their hands when they can hear what the child is saying. If they can't, have the child say the sentence a little louder and gradually increase the volume of his or her voice until everyone can hear.

SCRIPTURE

John 11:41

TALK

Alma and his people were in trouble. They were captured by the Lamanites and some wicked Nephites. The wicked Nephites told them they were not allowed to pray. But Alma and his people knew they needed to pray because they needed help. The people who captured them were making them work really hard. Alma's people were exhausted. They wanted to do what was right, but they were tired and scared.

Alma came up with a plan. He told his people that they should not pray out loud, but they should continue to pray in their hearts. Even though they didn't close their eyes or say the words with their mouths, the people continued to pray and exercise their faith.

Heavenly Father heard their silent prayers. He knew that they needed help and was glad that they were faithful. He gave them extra strength so they could do the hard work without getting tired. When the time was right, he helped Alma and the people escape and travel to the land of Zarahemla, where they could be safe.

Even when we cannot pray out loud, Heavenly Father hears us when we pray in our hearts. He will answer our prayers when we stay faithful.

LESSON

Discussion: Tell the children that Heavenly Father always hears our prayers. He loves us and is never too busy to listen to us when we pray.

- What does it mean to pray always?
- What does it mean to keep a prayer in your heart?

ACTIVITY

Read Alma 34:19–27 together. Explain that Amulek was teaching the people that they could pray anywhere about anything. Read the verses again, this time replacing the word *cry* with the word *pray*. Then go through the verses together a final time but pause at each blank space in the passage below and replace the word(s) in the verse with something the children could relate to. (For example, you could replace *fields* with *park* or *flocks* with *friends*.)

19 Yea, humble yourselves, and continue in prayer unto him.

20 Pray unto him when ye are in _____ (name a location), yea, over all your _____ (name something a child might be concerned about).

21 Pray unto him in your _____ (another location), yea, over all your _____ (another concern), both morning, mid-day, and evening.

22 Yea, pray unto him against the power of _____ (name something that could tempt them).

23 Yea, pray unto him against the devil, who is an enemy to all righteousness.

24 Pray unto him over _____ (something the children might be working on), that ye may prosper in them.

25 Pray over _____ (something the children want to have more of), that they may increase.

26 But this is not all; ye must pour out your souls in your _____ (another location), and your _____ (another location), and in your _____ (another location).

27 Yea, and when you do not pray unto the Lord, let your hearts be full, drawn out in prayer unto him continually for _____ (something the children need), and also for _____ (the same need) of/for _____ (a group of people).

If you have time beforehand, you may want to create a poster with this passage and draw pictures to illustrate the blank spots as you fill them in together. If you do not have time, you could write the verses on the board, or simply complete the activity verbally.

APPLICATION

Challenge the children to say at least one prayer this week in a place or at a time that they don't normally pray. They may decide to pray while in the car or while working on their homework. Encourage them to learn how to shut out any distractions around them and focus on communicating with their Heavenly Father.

REVIEW

Share an experience you have had when you said a prayer without praying out loud. Testify that Heavenly Father hears our prayers, no matter when or where we pray. Express your gratitude for the fact that Heavenly Father hears all our prayers.

Week 4: Heavenly Father Answers My Prayers

ATTENTION ACTIVITY

Write the following sentence on the board: "One time, Heavenly Father answered my prayer by _____." Invite a few of the teachers to come to the front of the room and finish the sentence by talking about an experience from their childhoods. If time permits and the children are interested, you could invite a few of them to complete the sentence as well.

SCRIPTURE

D&C 112:10

TALK

Most of the people in Babylon did not believe in Heavenly Father. They worshipped other things, like idols. But Daniel, one of the king's friends, believed in Heavenly Father. The king's other friends were jealous of Daniel. They came up with a plan to get rid of him. They told the king that he should make a law that everyone had to pray to the king and not to anyone else—including Heavenly Father.

After the law was passed, Daniel continued to pray to Heavenly Father. He knew that it was more important to obey Heavenly Father than the king. When the king's other friends found out, they told the king that Daniel was breaking the law. The king was sad. The punishment for not obeying the law was being put in a den of lions. The king did not want the lions to kill Daniel.

When Daniel was put in the lion's den, a miracle happened. The lions did not hurt him. Heavenly Father had saved Daniel because he prayed. The king was so happy that Daniel was okay. The king made a new law that everyone should respect Heavenly Father because He had saved Daniel.

LESSON

Discussion: Explain that Heavenly Father always answers our prayers, but sometimes we might not understand the answer at first, or we may need to wait for the answer. Other times, we may not recognize that our prayers were answered until much later because we did not recognize the answers when they came. And many times, Heavenly Father uses other people to answer our prayers so that they have an opportunity to serve us.

- What are some different ways Heavenly Father has answered your prayers?
- How can we learn to recognize the answers Heavenly Father sends us?

ACTIVITY

Read the following stories to the children. After each one, ask them, "How could Heavenly Father answer this prayer?" Try to come up with two or three answers for each scenario. At least one of these answers should include Heavenly Father using someone else to answer the prayer.

Maude really wants a new science kit for her birthday. She knows it is expensive, so she prays that Heavenly Father will bless her parents with enough money to buy the kit for her.

Parker is about to turn eight. He prays to know if he should be baptized.

Isaak knows that he should study for the test he has coming up at school, but he decides to play on his phone instead. Right before the test, he says a prayer that he will do well.

Eliza lost her favorite necklace at the park. She prays for help in finding it.

Beatrice wants to know if the bad things her friends told her about the Church are true. She prays to know the truth and hopes that Heavenly Father will appear to her the way He did to Joseph Smith.

Garrett is worried about his older brother, who is about to leave on a mission. Garrett prays that his brother will travel safely and be a good missionary.

APPLICATION

Explain that sometimes Heavenly Father expects us to be patient when we ask for answers. Watch "Continue in Patience"—YouTube, Mormon Channel, 2:41 (https://www.youtube.com/watch?v=654QGjY HlJY), or summarize the marshmallow experiment mentioned in Elder Uchtdorf's talk "Continue in Patience" (*Ensign*, May 2010).

Help the children to understand that even if Heavenly Father does not answer our prayers right away, He will answer them in time. Have the children spend a few moments quietly thinking about their prayers and how they have been answered. As they are thinking, have the pianist play "A Child's Prayer" (12) softly.

REVIEW

Share your testimony that God always answers our prayers, though not always in the way we expect. Help the children understand that He knows what is best for us and that sometimes what is best for us is not what we *think* is best. Encourage the children to be patient when they are seeking answers to their prayers and to continue in faith until the answers come.

Chapter 11: November
I Can Show Love and Respect
by Being Reverent

MULTIMEDIA RESOURCES

"The Last Supper"—YouTube, Mormon Channel, 6:01 (https://www.youtube.com/watch?v=997ni1xcmKw)

"Love Is Spoken Here"—YouTube, Mormon Tabernacle Choir, 3:45 (https://www.youtube.com/watch?v=S39Z6PPC1FM)

"Teach Me to Walk in the Light (Music Video) - Mormon Tabernacle Choir"—YouTube, Mormon Tabernacle Choir, 4:03 (https://www.youtube.com/watch?v=kK7XnmUzUUA)

"Encouraging Reverence"—LDS Media Library, 4:45 (https://www.lds.org/media-library/video/2012-03-1108-encouraging-reverence?lang=eng). Note: this is meant more for teachers and leaders than children.

SONG LIST

Focus Song: "When He Comes Again" (82)

Additional Songs: "Reverence Is Love" (31), "Saturday" (196), "The Chapel Doors" (156)

Review Songs: "If I Listen with My Heart," "I Will Follow God's Plan," "Stand for the Right," "Praise to the Man," "I Love to See the Temple," "The Lord Gave Me a Temple"

GOSPEL ART BOOK

"Passing the Sacrament" (108)

Week 1: I Will Show My Love and Respect by Being Reverent

ATTENTION ACTIVITY

Sing the song "Reverence Is Love" (31). If the children aren't familiar with this song, you may want to sing it a couple of times to help them understand its meaning.

SCRIPTURE

Leviticus 26:2

TALK

One Sunday, Adelaide's dad was giving a talk in sacrament meeting. Adelaide was so excited to see him up there that she kept waving to him while he was talking, but he didn't wave back. Her mom whispered to her that she needed to be more reverent. When they got home, her parents explained that waving in sacrament meeting could distract people from feeling the Spirit.

They told Adelaide that it's okay to be excited about things, but at church, we need to show respect to Heavenly Father because we are in His house. We can show respect for Heavenly Father by folding our arms to help us be still and quiet, like when we pray. We can also show respect by listening and answering questions politely during lessons.

Now Adelaide knows what it means to be reverent. She knows that feeling the Spirit is important and wants to help others feel it at church. More important, she wants to show Heavenly Father how much she loves Him by being reverent when it's time to think about holy things.

LESSON

Discussion: Help the children understand what it means to be reverent. Explain that reverence shows respect and love. Ask them to think about the coolest thing they've ever created. Maybe they took a long time working on a particular project for school or coloring a picture that they're especially proud of.

- How would you feel if someone stepped on your project? Or ripped it up?

Read 1 Nephi 19:7. Explain that Heavenly Father is not happy when we disregard sacred things or fail to give them the respect they deserve.

- How does being reverent show Heavenly Father that you're grateful for the things He has given you?

ACTIVITY

Play reverence charades. Invite one or two children to the front to act out one of the following reverent behaviors. Have the other children guess what the children in front are doing to be reverent.

- folding arms or hands to pray
- sitting still
- raising a hand to answer a question
- reading a scripture out loud
- walking quietly in the halls
- greeting friends reverently, even when you're excited to see them
- shaking hands with the missionaries
- helping to put away chairs or hymn books
- paying tithing
- singing a hymn or song in Primary
- picking up trash to keep the church clean
- taking the sacrament reverently
- smiling as you pass someone in the hallway
- taking care of your scriptures
- volunteering to help your teacher
- visiting the temple grounds with your family
- waiting patiently for a turn at the drinking fountain
- showing someone who is new where to go at church

APPLICATION

Have the children think of ways that they could show more reverence at church. Help them make a list of ideas on the board. Encourage them to pick one of the ideas and commit to working on it this month. Ask a few children to share their commitment with the group.

REVIEW

Share your own reverence commitment for the month. Tell the children about a time when you felt the Spirit or received revelation because you were being reverent. Express your appreciation for the children's reverence in class and tell them how it helps you to feel loved and respected.

Week 2: The Sacrament Is a Time to Remember Jesus

ATTENTION ACTIVITY

Display the following *Gospel Art Book* pictures in order around the room at the children's eye level. Tell them that today they are going to pretend to visit an art gallery and learn about an important series of events. Explain that in a real art gallery, the patrons are quiet, like in a library, so everyone there can experience the artwork. Have them reverently walk around the room and examine each picture at their own pace, identifying who is depicted and what is happening. When they are finished, ask them to return to their seats and think about what they have observed.

1. "Triumphal Entry" (50)
2. "The Last Supper" (54)
3. "Jesus Washing the Apostles' Feet" (55)
4. "Jesus Praying in Gethsemane" (56)
5. "The Crucifixion" (57)
6. "Burial of Jesus" (58)
7. "Mary and the Resurrected Jesus Christ" (59)
8. "Jesus Shows His Wounds" (60)

SCRIPTURE

Luke 22:19–20

TALK

On Sundays, Ethan's older brother Erik sits up front at the start of the meeting so he can help pass the sacrament. Ethan likes to watch his brother during the sacrament. He knows someday he will be able to help pass the sacrament too.

One Sunday, Ethan, Erik, and their dad went with some other young men in the ward to visit an old man. Ethan had never met the old man before because the man was so sick he had to stay in bed all the time. While they were there, they blessed the sacrament and helped the old man eat and drink it. It was not exactly the same as being in a chapel with lots of other people around. But it was special, and Ethan could feel the Spirit there.

Ethan is looking forward to receiving the priesthood so he can help pass the sacrament too. He knows that the sacrament is the most important part of our time at church each week. It is a time to remember Jesus and what we are doing to become more like Him.

LESSON

Discussion: If you didn't use the attention activity, have the children help you tell the story of Jesus's suffering in Gethsemane and on the cross. Continue the story with His Resurrection. If you used the attention activity, direct the children's attention back to the pictures around the room.

Explain that Jesus suffered so that we wouldn't have to. Tell them that during the sacrament, we should remember Jesus and the sacrifice He made for us. We should also think about the covenants we have made or will make someday.

- What does it mean to renew covenants?
- What kinds of things could you do or think about during the sacrament? (List these on the board.)

ACTIVITY

Have the children create sacrament books to look at during the sacrament. Bring paper and a stapler with you. Have the children fold two papers in half width-wise to create a booklet. Use the stapler to create a binding—or use another method if you prefer. Try to make sure each book has at least four pages. Have the children illustrate their books with pictures of the Savior. Older children may also wish to copy lyrics from their favorite sacrament hymn into their books.

APPLICATION

Help the children to practice being reverent by inviting one of the teachers to come forward and share a brief testimony of the Atonement. Tell the children that this is a chance for them to practice being as still and quiet as they would during the sacrament. If time permits, sing "He Sent His Son" (34) together.

REVIEW

Tell the children that Jesus did so many things for us. We can show Him that we love and appreciate all those things by spending a little

Time to Share

time each week thinking of Him during the sacrament. Encourage older children to remember their baptismal covenant during the sacrament and use that time to think over how they have kept that covenant throughout the preceding week and how they can improve in the week ahead. Bear your testimony that the Atonement is what allows us to change and become more like Jesus. Help the children understand that the sacrament is a time for quiet, joyful reflection as we ponder our personal course back to the Savior.

Week 3: I Will Show Respect for Sacred Places and Things

ATTENTION ACTIVITY

Bring something to show the children that is important to you or your family. It could be an heirloom or tool you use a lot—something that would be hard to live without. Explain that because this object is so important, you try to treat it carefully. You keep it safe and make sure that if someone else wants to use it, they know how to care for it properly.

SCRIPTURE

Alma 37:14

TALK

Kave loves the stories of Nephi and Lehi in the Book of Mormon. Sometimes he likes to pretend that he's building a ship, hunting animals with a bow and arrow in the wilderness, or protecting his people with the sword of Laban. But one of Kave's favorite parts is when Lehi finds the Liahona. Kave always wonders what the Liahona really looks like and if he'll have a special compass like that to guide him on his adventures.

Kave *does* have a special compass. It doesn't look like the Liahona. But Alma tells us that the word of God can be our Liahona today. That means Kave's scriptures and the words of our modern prophets can be like a compass on our journey back to Heavenly Father. And just like the Liahona, the scriptures only work like a compass when we pay attention to them, do what they say, and take good care of them.

Just as Nephi and Lehi had to take good care of the Liahona, the sword of Laban, their bows and arrows, and the brass plates, we have many special things we need to take care of today. Our temples need lots of care to keep them looking perfect. And the same is true for our scriptures, our church buildings, and other sacred things. But even more important is taking care of the things we cannot always see, like our families, testimonies, and relationship with Heavenly Father. We can take care of these things by treating them reverently, because reverence is a way to show respect and love.

LESSON

Discussion: Refer to the attention activity, if you used it. Talk about how things that are important need to be taken care of in the right way.

Time to Share

- What things are important to you?
- How does an attitude of reverence help us take better care of sacred things?

ACTIVITY

Explain to the children that there are many sacred places and things that need to be taken care of reverently. Some of them are things we can touch and see. Others are things we feel or ideas that we need to speak about respectfully.

For younger children: Assign each child one of the reverence items in the chart below. Have them draw a picture to illustrate it, and then have a few children hold up their pictures and discuss what we should do to show reverence for this item or idea.

For older children: Print or write out slips of paper with the following list of reverence items and activities on it. Cut the slips so that each one has a single item or activity. Put all of the slips of paper in a bowl or jar and have the children come up with their classmates to pick a piece of paper from the jar. When they return to their seats, have their teachers help them read their papers. Then tell them to walk around reverently and see if they can find the person whose reverence item matches their reverence activity, or vice versa.

Note: There may be multiple matches for some items and activities. This is okay as long as each item is paired with at least one activity.

Reverence Item	Reverence Activity
The scriptures	Handle them carefully; put them back when you are done reading
The temple	Help keep the grounds clean; prepare to go inside someday
The church building	Take turns cleaning it; walk reverently in the halls
Pictures of Jesus	Don't crumple them up or rip them
Heavenly Father's name	Say it respectfully—not lightly or in vain
The Sabbath day	Keep it holy
A hymn book	Put it back where it belongs when you are done singing

The chairs at church	Help put them away when class is over
The cultural hall	This can be a fun place to play, but always remember that you are still in a church building
Your eternal family	Treat each person kindly; serve them and love them
Prayers	Be quiet and still; say amen at the end
The sacrament	Take the bread and water reverently
Parents	Obey them; show them respect when they are speaking
Teachers	Listen carefully when they are teaching; help them with lessons and clean up
Sunday clothes	Wear nice clothes to church on Sunday; be careful not to get them dirty

You may need to have the children work in pairs or teams if you have a large Primary. If your Primary is smaller, print just part of each list.

APPLICATION

Ask the children to talk about a time when they felt the Spirit because they were being reverent. After a few children have shared, remind them of their commitments from two weeks ago. Ask them how they are doing. If they have forgotten what they wanted to work on to be more reverent in church, take this opportunity to have them recommit for the remainder of the month and perhaps write down their goals this time.

REVIEW

Tell the children how being reverent helps us feel more respect for Heavenly Father and the things He has given us. Discuss the idea of stewardship and how Heavenly Father has entrusted us with sacred things because He knows we will take good care of them. Emphasize how blessed we are to have a nice place to worship, wonderful families, and knowledge of the true gospel.

Week 4: Reverence Helps Me Love and Respect God and the People around Me

ATTENTION ACTIVITY

Sing both verses of "Jesus Wants Me for a Sunbeam" (60). You may need to teach the children the second verse.

SCRIPTURE

John 13:34

TALK

Erin is used to sharing. In her family, she feels like she has to share everything. Her brothers always want to play with her toys and games, and even the family dog begs Erin to give him a bite of whatever she's eating. Most of the time, Erin doesn't mind sharing. But there are some times when it becomes extra hard.

One time, she and her dad were supposed to have a special day, just the two of them. But at the last minute, her little brother had to come too because he got sick and couldn't stay with the babysitter. Erin was sad that she had to share the time she spent with her dad that day.

In Heavenly Father's family, we have to share too. Each of us is a child of God, and He loves us, but He expects us to share what we have with all our brothers and sisters and treat them kindly. This means we need to look out for those who have fewer blessings and try to help them. We also need to share our time in serving those who have particular needs. Sometimes it can be hard to share and serve others, but when we understand that all people on earth are our brothers or sisters, we will feel love for them and want to share what we have to bless them.

LESSON

Discussion: Tell the children that being kind is a way to show reverence because when we are reverent and respectful, we care more about others than we do about ourselves. Explain that when Jesus lived on earth, He cared for everyone—even the people others did not respect.

- Why is it important to be kind to everybody?
- How is being kind to someone else like being kind to Heavenly Father or Jesus?

ACTIVITY

Watch the video "Parables of Jesus: Parable of the Good Samaritan" —YouTube, Mormon Channel, 5:11 (https://www.youtube.com/watch?v=53Pqw20xK10).

APPLICATION

Explain that we need to love everybody because every person we meet is a son or daughter of God. Heavenly Father wants us to treat each of His children kindly. This means we should never intentionally hurt someone else with the things we do, think, or say.

Have the children think about ways they could show love or respect for their neighbors. Then have them turn to each of the children sitting next to them and finish the sentence, "I will be kind to you by _____."

REVIEW

Share with the children your testimony of how much Heavenly Father loves His children and how sad He is when we don't treat each other well. Tell them that being kind to others shows Heavenly Father you love Him and respect all His children. Express your feelings about one way that someone has been kind to you recently.

Chapter 12: December

The Scriptures Tell of Jesus's Birth and Second Coming

MULTIMEDIA RESOURCES

"The Nativity"—YouTube, Mormon Channel, 7:52 (https://www.youtube.com/watch?v=YijgnaGk2Us)

"Kids & Christmas - Learning the Meaning of Christmas through The Eyes of Children"—YouTube, Mormon Channel, 2:48 (https://www.youtube.com/watch?v=RM8XoT7qnxY)

"The Greatest Gift"—YouTube, LDS Youth, 1:45 (https://www.youtube.com/watch?v=D3-T-bm78Xc)

"What Shall We Give?"—YouTube, Mormon Channel, 3:51 (https://www.youtube.com/watch?v=0FSQuHDIsVw)

"Chapter 19: The Second Coming of Jesus Christ"—YouTube, Mormon Channel, 3:02 (https://www.youtube.com/watch?v=NNalljDgak4)

SONG LIST

Focus Song: "When He Comes Again" (82)

Additional Songs: "Picture a Christmas" (50), "Away in a Manger" (42), "Once within a Lowly Stable" (41)

Review Songs: "If I Listen with My Heart," "I Will Follow God's Plan," "Stand for the Right," "Praise to the Man," "I Love to See the Temple," "The Lord Gave Me a Temple"

GOSPEL ART BOOK

"The Second Coming" (66)

Week 1: Prophets Foretold Jesus's Birth

ATTENTION ACTIVITY

Ask a few children to share some good news or something that they are excited about. Explain that before Jesus was born, those who knew He was coming were very excited. They wanted to tell everyone about Jesus because His birth was the best news.

SCRIPTURE

Jacob 7:11

TALK

Olivia is so excited for Christmas! She can't wait to open up her presents on Christmas morning and find out what she got. She wishes she could find out what her presents are now, before Christmas. She tries asking her mom for hints about her gifts, but her mom tells her that would ruin the surprise.

Of course, Olivia knows that the real reason we celebrate Christmas is to help us remember Christ. His life and death for us are the greatest gift we will ever receive. And His gift was not a surprise. Many people knew about Jesus before He was born.

These people were called prophets, and they knew a lot about Jesus. They knew where He would be born and what He would be named. They knew He would perform miracles and teach the people. And they knew He would die to save us all. The prophets told the people in their times about Jesus so that everyone could look forward to the Savior's gift and believe in Him.

LESSON

Discussion: Ask the children how they know the story of Jesus's birth. Explain that we know Jesus was born in Bethlehem because we have the scriptures to tell us about what happened many years ago. Tell them that before Jesus was born, there were no scriptures to tell the story because it hadn't happened yet. But many people still knew the story because prophets had seen visions and told the people what would happen.

- Why was it important for people to know about Jesus before He was born?

- How many prophets can you think of who told their people about Jesus before His birth?

ACTIVITY

Write the words *who, what, where, when,* and *why* on the board. Then write the numbers one through five. Invite a child to come up and choose one of the numbers. Help the child in front read the corresponding scripture from the list below and have the other children identify which question that verse answers and what that prophesy foretold about Jesus. When you finish the discussion, have the child in front erase that number. Repeat the process until you have discussed all five questions and prophecies.

1. Helaman 14:5 (what): A new star would appear when Jesus was born.
2. 1 Nephi 11:18–20 (who): A virgin (Mary) would have a son (Jesus).
3. Helaman 5:9 (why): Jesus would come to redeem the world.
4. Micah 5:2 (where): Jesus would be born in Bethlehem.
5. 1 Nephi 19:8 (when): Jesus's birth would happen six hundred years after Lehi left Jerusalem.

APPLICATION

Explain to the children that just like ancient prophets told their people about Jesus, modern prophets still teach us about Him. They help us learn about the commandments and how to live them in our day. Ask the children if they know of any recent counsel from modern prophets. Encourage them to view the First Presidency Christmas Devotional with their families.

REVIEW

Help the children understand that many people knew about Jesus before He was born. They looked forward to the day when He would come to the earth and knew that His Atonement would save them from sin and death. They were faithful and full of hope. We can be faithful like they were and obey the prophets in our day. Share your appreciation for the Savior and for modern prophets, who serve as special witnesses of Him.

Week 2: Jesus Was Born on the Earth

ATTENTION ACTIVITY

Bring a small Nativity set or show pictures of each figure. Invite a few children to come to the front and hold up the pieces as you briefly tell them about each one.

SCRIPTURE

Isaiah 9:6

TALK

Simeon was an old man. He lived righteously and had the Holy Ghost with him. The Holy Ghost told him that he would see the Savior before he died. Simeon was faithful. He waited a long time.

Then one day, the Holy Ghost sent Simeon a prompting. The Holy Ghost told Simeon to go to the temple. He obeyed. While Simeon was at the temple, he saw a couple come in with a newborn baby. Immediately, Simeon knew who they were. He knew that the baby was Jesus and that someday Jesus would be the Savior.

Simeon went over to the couple, Mary and Joseph. He held Jesus in his arms and praised God. He told Heavenly Father he was grateful he had seen Jesus. Then Simeon prophesied that Jesus would save everyone. Joseph and Mary were amazed at the things Simeon said. They all knew that Jesus had a special mission to perform. He would change the world forever.

LESSON

Discussion: Read 1 Nephi 11:16–20. Explain that Nephi saw a vision of Jesus's birth. He saw that Jesus would be born as a mortal baby on the earth. Jesus grew up and learned in the same way that we do, except that He didn't make any mistakes.

- What does it mean to condescend?
- Why did Jesus choose to be born in a lowly stable instead of somewhere beautiful or more clean?

ACTIVITY

Watch "The Nativity"—YouTube, Mormon Channel, 7:52 (https://www.youtube.com/watch?v=YijgnaGk2Us)

APPLICATION

Tell the children that just like the shepherds spread the wonderful news of Jesus's birth, we can share what we know about Jesus with others this Christmas season. Work together to create a list of ideas that the children could do to invite others to learn about Jesus. This might include inviting a friend to a Christmas activity, giving a Book of Mormon as a gift, or bearing testimony at a family gathering.

REVIEW

Testify of Jesus's divinity. Help the children learn that He chose to experience the pains and sorrows of this world as a mortal man so that He would be able to understand how we feel. Express your feelings about Christmastime and the gift that Jesus gave to each of us through the Atonement.

Week 3: Jesus Will Come Again Someday

ATTENTION ACTIVITY

Draw or display photos of a few road signs. Ask the children what they mean. Explain that when we are driving, signs tell us what is coming up on the road ahead. Before Jesus comes again, there will be signs that help us know He is coming. Some of those signs have already appeared.

SCRIPTURE

Matthew 25:31

TALK

Jasmine lives in a farmhouse in the middle of a big field. Most of the time in the summer, the weather is nice and sunny. But sometimes, there are storms that come in. Jasmine can always tell when a storm is coming because certain things happen first. Right before a big storm, the animals on the farm start to get restless. Jasmine helps her parents make sure they are safe. The wind starts blowing. Jasmine likes to go inside to watch the patterns the wind makes in the fields from a window. From there, she can see the storm clouds gathering. They are dark and heavy. Sometimes Jasmine can spot lightning in the distance. Just before the storm hits, the wind stops. Then it starts raining, or even hailing.

The animals, wind, clouds, and lightning all act as signs to let Jasmine know a storm is coming. Jesus gave all of us signs to look for before His Second Coming. He revealed these signs to His prophets, and they have written them in our scriptures for us to read. Some of these signs have already happened, and that means we can be excited because we know that Jesus really will return someday.

LESSON

Discussion: Refer back to the attention activity, if you used it. Read Matthew 24:32–33. Explain that Jesus has told us about signs that will herald or foretell His coming.

- Do you know any of these signs?
- What does it mean to live in the latter days, or last days?

ACTIVITY

Help the children identify some signs of the Second Coming by randomly displaying on the board the *Gospel Art Book* pictures from the chart below. Invite one of the children to read the scripture references for one of the signs, or simply read the scriptures aloud yourself. Ask the children to identify which picture depicts the sign you read about. Once they guess correctly, write the name of the sign below that picture. Ask them if this sign has already happened and discuss how it was fulfilled or how it will be fulfilled someday.

Illustration	Scripture References	Sign	Has This Happened?
"Two Thousand Young Warriors" (80)	Matthew 24:6–7 (see also D&C 88:90)	Wars and calamities	While some destruction has happened, this sign will continue to intensify until the Second Coming.
"Moroni Appears to Joseph Smith in His Room" (91)	Revelation 14:6–7 (see also) D&C 45:28	Restoration of the gospel	Yes. The Prophet Joseph Smith was visited by angels, including the angel Moroni, who helped him restore the fulness of the gospel in our day.
"Joseph Smith Translating the Book of Mormon" (92)	Ezekiel 37:16–20 (see also Isaiah 29:4–18)	Emergence of the Book of Mormon	Yes. The Prophet Joseph Smith translated the Book of Mormon, and it is now being shared across the world.
"Missionaries: Elders" (109); "Missionaries: Sisters" (110)	Matthew 24:14; (see also D&C 90:11)	The gospel is preached to all the world	There are many places the gospel has been preached, but there are still others where good people are waiting to hear the truth.
"Elijah Appearing in the Kirtland Temple" (95)	Malachi 4:5–6	The coming of Elijah	Yes. Elijah appeared to Joseph Smith and Oliver Cowdery in the Kirtland Temple. Elijah restored the priesthood power to seal families together for eternity.

Time to Share

Illustration	Scripture References	Sign	Has This Happened?
"Christ and Children from around the World" (116)	3 Nephi 21:23–25 (see also Moses 7:62–64; Articles of Faith 1:10)	The building of the New Jerusalem	No. This city will one day be built in Missouri (see D&C 84:2–3).

Note: Much of this chart was adapted from the *Gospel Principles Manual Lesson 43* (*Gospel Principles* [2011], 251–56).

APPLICATION

Explain to the children that though we don't know when Jesus will come again, there are some things we can do to prepare. We can share the gospel with others so that they will be ready. We can make sure that our families are prepared by having a plan in case of emergencies. Encourage the children to discuss their emergency plans with their families this week.

REVIEW

Help the children understand that they do not need to be afraid of the signs that will come before Jesus returns. Instead, we need to prepare ourselves to see Him again, live righteously, and repent. If we do those things, we can happily look forward to the day when our Savior will return and everyone will live in peace.

Week 4: I Can Prepare for the Second Coming by Following Jesus's Example

ATTENTION ACTIVITY

Watch "I'm Trying to Be like Jesus (Music Video) - Mormon Tabernacle Choir"—YouTube, Mormon Tabernacle Choir, 5:16 (https://www.youtube.com/watch?v=oe2HZuEZG6I). Ask the children to listen for the line that mentions Jesus coming again. Have them raise their hands when they hear it.

SCRIPTURE

D&C 38:30–31

TALK

Jesus told a story about a man who had a lot of money, called *talents*. When the man had to leave for a while, he gave some talents to his three servants to take care of while he was gone. Two of the servants used the money to make more money by doing business, but one servant was so afraid of losing the money that he just hid his talent so it wouldn't get lost.

Then one day, the man returned. He asked his servants what they had done with the money he'd given them. He was pleased to find that two of the servants had made more money. He was not happy that one servant had kept his talent hidden the whole time.

In this story, the man with the money represents Jesus and we are the servants. Jesus has given us many opportunities to work hard and become better people. But we do not know when we will see Him again. We need to be like the servants who worked hard to make more money and prepare now for Jesus to come again by being kind to others, sharing the gospel, and making good choices.

LESSON

Discussion: Tell the children that today you will be talking about an exciting surprise that is going to happen someday. Have them guess what this surprise could be. After a few guesses, explain that the surprise is Jesus's Second Coming. For many years, prophets and faithful saints have looked forward to Jesus's return.

Time to Share

- How do we know that Jesus will return someday?
- What should we do to get ready for the Second Coming?

ACTIVITY

Explain to the children that because we do not know when Jesus will return, we need to always be ready. Play a game of freeze, in which the pianist plays brief sections of a Primary song while the children reverently move around the room. (You may consider using the song "When He Comes Again" [82].) Tell the children that when the music stops, they should immediately freeze and hold still until it begins again.

When the song is over, have the children return to their seats. Read Matthew 24:42 and discuss the idea that just as the children did not know when the music would stop, we do not know when Christ will return. Help them understand that we need to always be ready for the Savior's return by doing all we can to prepare each day.

APPLICATION

Refer to the talk, if one of the children gave it. If not, summarize the parable of the talents (see Matthew 25:14–29). Give each child one "talent"—this could be a sticker, a small piece of paper, or a penny. Tell them that their job during the week is to turn their single talent into more talents by serving others and making good choices. Ask them to have their parents help them write down one good thing they did each day. Instruct them to bring their papers to church the next week. If they bring their papers the following week, be prepared to give them more "talents" for each of the days on which they made and recorded a good choice or deed.

REVIEW

Explain to the children that we should joyfully look forward to the Second Coming. Help them to understand that when Jesus comes again, we will be happy to see Him. Everyone on earth will know that He sacrificed Himself for us, and we will all live in peace. Testify that you know Christ will return someday and share your commitment to prepare for the Second Coming.

Singing Time

Singing time is meant to help children learn the gospel through music. Though this chapter will include some basic instructions on vocal music, the purpose of singing time is not to create the most beautiful or even the most harmonious choir of young voices. Rather, it is to help children internalize gospel truths and create a doctrinal foundation that they can draw upon for years to come. And it's just fun!

This chapter is divided into activities that will work for any song, specific ideas for the songs you will feature in the Primary Program for 2016, and some general vocal and music instruction tips.

ACTIVITIES FOR ANY SONG

Depending on what you're trying to teach during singing time, you may consider some of the following activities. Keep in mind that while they can be fun, the use of elaborate props, costumes, or visuals is not necessary and can even be distracting. The following simple activities do not require much prep time and will work with any songs you choose to sing.

Activities for Memorization and Learning

There'll be times, particularly as you prepare for the annual Primary Program, when you will want the children to learn a song well or even memorize it as a Primary class. Using a mix of the following activities will help emphasize these songs while keeping them fresh from week to week.

- Repeat one line at a time until the children have mastered it.
- Write a verse on the board and erase a few words at a time.
- Stop mid-song and ask the children what words come next.
- Have the teachers drop out in the middle of a verse.
- Make cards with the lyrics and mix them up. Have the children sort them out and display them on the board, or have children hold the cards and stand in order at the front of the room.
- Speak the words together slowly before singing.
- Clap the rhythm of the song to help them learn the timing.
- Ask children to raise their hands and speak or sing one line at a time. When the first child finishes the first line, ask a second child to speak or sing the second line, and so on.

Activities for Movement

These activities are perfect when you need to get the wiggles out of a rambunctious group or energize one that is starting to lag. With these activities, you will want to observe the children closely to make sure that they are still being reverent even when they're having fun.

- Have the children listen for certain words and stand up whenever they sing those words.
- Have half the room stand and sing, while the other half sits and hums. Partway through a line or verse, point to the side of the room that is sitting. This means that the sitting group should stand and sing while the other group sits and hums. Continue switching back and forth whenever you point to one side or the other.
- Create actions for specific words or phrases. (See the next section on the Primary Program songs for some examples and ideas.)
- Have the children slowly walk in a circle around the room as they sing.
- Let the children wiggle in their seats as they sing, and then have the pianist stop playing suddenly. Tell the children that when the music stops, they should freeze until it begins again.
- Invite one child to the front of the room to move around reverently as he or she sings. Instruct the other children to try to match the movements of the child in front.

- Pick a word in the lyrics and have the children stand up and shout when they sing that word.

Activities for Emphasizing Doctrine

- Have the children hum along to the tune as you read the words to them, pointing out important thoughts or ideas.
- Have older children write the words down and younger ones draw pictures to help them remember what the words mean.
- Give each class a line of the lyrics and have them explain what it means to everyone.
- Play a recording of the song and pause after each verse to discuss its meaning.
- Have the children plan a music video for this song and ask them what kinds of shots or illustrations they would want to feature for each line of the song.

SPECIFIC IDEAS AND ACTIVITIES FOR THE PRIMARY PROGRAM SONGS

"If I Listen with My Heart": The three verses of this song reference three ways we can hear the Savior speaking to us. Consider using the scriptures as a visual reminder of verse one, a picture of the prophet for verse two, and pointing to your head and heart for verse three to represent the Holy Ghost. Sample actions for verse 1:

- Line 1: "little"—place hand palm down at waist height
- Line 2: "walk"—walk in place or move fingers across arm to show walking
- Line 3: "scriptures"—open hands like a book
- Line 4: "heart"—place hands over heart

You could ask the children to help you come up with additional actions for the second and third verses.

"I Will Follow God's Plan": Because this song does not have a chorus or repeated sections, it is a good one to learn one line at a time.

Try having the children point to themselves anytime they sing the words *my*, *me*, or *I*.

This is a good song to teach phrasing and breathing techniques because the phrases are short and broken up. You may want to try having one class sing the first phrase, then the next class could sing the next phrase, and so on.

Time to Share

"Stand for the Right": As you're practicing, you could have the children say the words, "Be true, be true" loudly instead of singing them.

You could also have them stand up as they sing the word *stand* in the last line. And they could point to the front of the room or to you as they sing the word *you* in the first line.

This is a good song for teaching rhythm. You may want to practice clapping out the beat a few times with the children before singing it.

"Praise to the Man": This hymn may look daunting for a Primary at first glance, but many children will already be familiar with the tune because it is the same one used for "The Books in the New Testament" (116).

You might wish to try beginning with the chorus before learning the individual verses. That way, you can fall back on something familiar at the end of each verse. The key to this song will be to help the children understand the words they are singing. The following is a list of words and simple definitions that you will want to explain as you sing them. They are listed in the order they would be sung, with the chorus after the first verse and the subsequent verses following.

- Communed—communicated with
- Anointed—gave a special mission to
- Dispensation—a period of gospel learning
- Extol him—talk about how great he is
- Nations revere—people from all over the world will respect him
- Ascended—gone up
- Tyrants—people who want power and control
- Mingling—talking to and living with
- Conquer—have power over
- Martyr—someone who dies for their faith
- Assassins—people who kill others for selfish reasons
- Lauds—applauds, praises
- Midst—middle
- Atone—make up for
- Conflict—struggle
- Justice—righteousness

You could write out the lyrics for this song, writing the words above in red. Then have the children sing until they reach a red word. Stop there to make sure they understand that word before continuing.

"I Love to See the Temple": Many children will already know this song, so it is a good one for teaching dynamics. In each line, you could pick a key word or two to emphasize. Build in volume leading up to this word, then fall in volume after.

Example: I love to see the *temple* / I'm *going* there someday / To feel the *Holy Spirit* / To *listen* and to *pray*.

You might also consider having the children learn the American Sign Language signs that accompany this song. You can find a video of the signs, available for download, on lds.org.

"The Lord Gave Me a Temple": The first verse of this song repeats the word *temple* several times. You may want to have the children use an action for this word by putting their hands together to form a peaked roof. They could also use this action for the word *home* in line two. Another word that is repeated is *body*. You could have them lift their arms in the air whenever you sing this word or use another action to help them remember it.

This song's rhythm is unique. You may want to practice saying the words to the beat a few times, or have the children clap the rhythm before they sing.

BASIC MUSICALITY AND VOCAL TIPS FOR PRIMARY SINGERS

Posture and breathing: Help the children to practice good posture as they sing by encouraging them to sit up straight in their chairs or to stand with feet shoulder width apart. Have them imagine that someone is pulling them up by a string from the tops of their heads. Their shoulders should be back and their chests forward, ready to breathe deeply. Try having them insert three fingers into their mouths to feel how open their jaws should be as they pronounce vowels.

Encourage them to breathe deeply and use their diaphragms to regulate their breathing. You may wish to have them place their hands at the bottom of their rib cages to feel where their diaphragms are. Have them use this muscle to control their volume and breathing.

You could consider helping them to focus with a simple warm-up such as deeply inhaling through their noses for four counts, and then slowly exhaling on a hiss.

Phrasing and dynamics: These two elements of a song can have a major impact when it comes to the message of the lyrics. In general, try to keep phrases intact by teaching the children to breathe at the end of a phrase, or when a comma or period comes up in the lyrics rather than at random. For example, in the hymn "Praise to the Man," you may decide not to include a breath after the word *tyrants* in the chorus.

Use the Spirit as you consider the dynamics of a song you would like the children to sing. Some songs may call for a more reverent or thoughtful tone, while others may be better for rejoicing. Teach the children to emphasize important words by changing the volume at which they sing them.

Musical terms: Depending on your own musical background, you may choose to teach the children a few musical terms. Because they will likely not be reading the music as they sing, you don't need to worry about teaching them the different notes or rests, but you may want to tell them why a rest would be used.

You might also consider having them learn the difference in sound between a major and a minor chord, as well as why a composer might choose to use one versus another. In general, you will want to emphasize how the different musical elements of a song work together to enhance its message.

Teaching the children how to lead music: Older children especially may enjoy learning how to lead music. You can refer to the "Using the Hymnbook" section of *Hymns* for specific information on the different beat patterns (see specifically pages 384–85). In general, learning to lead music and stay on beat can help children learn the tempo of a song. While they may not be ready to actually lead a group, they might enjoy leading all together with you as everyone sings.

This is a skill that they can begin practicing now to use in Aaronic Priesthood quorums or Young Women's classes.

Primary Program

The annual Primary sacrament meeting presentation is an opportunity for you and the children in Primary to share what you are learning with the rest of the ward. Elaborate visuals, costumes, or videos are not appropriate for sacrament meeting. Focus instead on bringing the Spirit with music and simple testimonies. Try to keep your expectations age appropriate. Younger children may only be able to memorize a short line. On the other hand, you can keep older children engaged by asking them to perform some of the songs in small groups or give longer talks. Organizing the children by their classes could help them to know when it will be their turn to speak.

This chapter begins with some general tips and ideas for preparing and giving your program. After this section, you'll find a sample outline for the program that you can adapt to the needs of your children.

PREPARING FOR YOUR PRESENTATION

In addition to having the children practice the songs and speaking parts, you will want to have them practice reverence on the stand, how to conduct themselves during the meeting, and how to speak into the microphone correctly. To this end, you may want to plan to have the Primary give a special musical number in sacrament meeting in August or even July. This will give you a chance to teach the children how to reverently walk to the front of the chapel, assemble themselves to sing, and project their voices. You could also try introducing a microphone in sharing time and have the children who participate in the lesson that day try using the microphone to answer questions or read scriptures. You could also come up with a simple hand symbol for reverence that you use in your Primary. Make sure the children know what it is and what it means so you can use it to signal to them nonverbally during the program and practices.

Practices for the presentation shouldn't take away unnecessarily from family time. If you have a large Primary, you might consider breaking your practices into sessions for junior and senior Primary. You might also think about providing coloring pages or some other quiet activity to younger children to keep them occupied while the older ones are practicing their parts. In general, it is best to practice special musical numbers, like those performed by only one child or one class, separately so as not to waste the time of the larger group.

If you plan to have the children sit on the stand for the entire meeting, you will want to plan a seating arrangement that ensures reverence. If necessary, separate children who can't sit next to each other without distracting others. Be strategic in where you place teachers.

Have the children practice standing and making their way to the microphone reverently. If possible, give the children their parts as early as possible so they have time to learn them before the presentation. Don't worry about perfection as you are practicing, and avoid stopping the presentation to fix little things. The point is to help the children get used to the overall flow of the meeting.

SAMPLE PRESENTATION IDEAS

It's a good idea to begin the presentation with a short introduction from a member of the Primary presidency. You could say something like,

> This year in Primary, we are learning about the scriptures and how they help us grow closer to Heavenly Father and Jesus Christ. Each month, we have focused on a new gospel topic and used the scriptures to help us understand what Heavenly Father wants us to know. Some of these topics include the plan of salvation, the role of prophets, the Restoration, temples, missionary work, and prayer. Today, we are excited to present what we have learned about these topics to you. We know that the scriptures can give us strength to withstand temptation and help us build God's kingdom. We know the scriptures are true and hope you have a testimony of them too.

You may want to have an older child or group of older children act as narrators throughout the program, introducing each new monthly topic. Alternatively, you could ask one of the teachers or leaders to fill this role. The remainder of this sample outline will follow the structure below.

Topic: A simple introduction that could be given by a teacher or narrator.

- sample line for young children
- sample part for older children
- idea for a talk from one older child

You do not need to include both older and younger children for each topic. Use the Spirit to help you create a structure and presentation that works for the children in your Primary. If possible, leave time at the end of the program for a member of the bishopric to offer some brief remarks.

SAMPLE OUTLINE

Introduction from Primary presidency (see above).

Song: "If I Listen with My Heart"

The scriptures: We know that Heavenly Father speaks to us through the scriptures. We love learning scripture stories, and we are grateful for the truths we find in them.

- My favorite scripture hero is _____.
- Nephi tells us to liken the scriptures to ourselves. This means we need to learn to apply the scriptures to our lives. I have learned to do this by following the examples of my favorite scripture heroes when I feel discouraged or tempted to make a bad choice. Sometimes, I imagine what they would choose if they were me. I try to choose what they would choose.
- You could have one of the older children speak about a favorite scripture passage or scripture story. Have the child share the verse or verses, and then explain how those verses have helped the child find strength or to face a specific situation in the child's life.

Heavenly Father's plan: We learn in the scriptures that Heavenly Father has a plan for each of us. This plan is called the plan of salvation, or the plan of happiness. We know that if we follow the plan, we can live with Heavenly Father again.

Time to Share

- I want to follow Heavenly Father's plan.
- I know that I lived with Heavenly Father before I was born. I made choices there and learned new things. I chose to come to earth to gain a body and continue learning.
- You could have an older child give an overview of the plan of salvation, including where we lived before we were born, the purpose of our time on earth, and what will happen to our bodies and our spirits after we die. Have the child share how having an eternal perspective changes the way we live our lives.

Song: "I Will Follow God's Plan"

Prophets: Prophets teach us how to follow Jesus. In the scriptures, we can read about lots of prophets who lived in the past. We are grateful to also have modern prophets who help us know what to do today.

- I love listening to the prophet.
- Prophets warn and protect the people they lead. Moses helped his people escape from slavery in Egypt. Brigham Young led all the pioneers across the plains. I know that our prophet today leads us and teaches us how to choose the right.
- An older child could talk about an experience he or she had sustaining the prophet by following his counsel, even when it was difficult. Have him or her testify that prophets know what we need, and they will never lead us astray.

Song: "Stand for the Right"

Jesus's life and Atonement: In the scriptures, we can read about Jesus's life and the example He set. We can also learn about His Atonement. We know that He loved us and gave His life so that we can live again with Him someday.

- I know that Jesus loves me.
- Jesus set the perfect example for me. I am trying to follow Him by being kind to others, learning the gospel, and sharing good things with the people around me. I am grateful for the Atonement and how it helps me to change.
- You could have an older child talk about what the Atonement means to him or her or how he or she has already begun using it to repent. Ask the child to share how it feels to know that Jesus willingly suffered for us because He loves us more than He loves Himself.

The Restoration: When Joseph Smith restored the true Church, he brought us new scriptures that are meant for our day. He translated the Book of Mormon and parts of the Bible. He also recorded many new revelations in the Doctrine and Covenants.

- Joseph Smith taught about the temple.
- When Joseph Smith was a young man, he prayed to know which church was true. Heavenly Father and Jesus appeared to him. They told him he would need to restore the true Church.
- Have an older child testify of the truthfulness of the Book of Mormon. You will want to have the child share how he or she gained a personal testimony of it and how this testimony has helped him or her know that Joseph Smith is a true prophet in our day.

Song: "Praise to the Man"

The first principles and ordinances of the gospel: We know that the first principles and ordinances of the gospel will help us to come closer to Jesus. We can read about them in the scriptures, especially in the fourth article of faith.

- I have faith in Heavenly Father and Jesus.
- Repenting means trying to change. When I do something wrong, I know that I can be forgiven if I try to make up for my mistake and I really feel sorry. I also know that I need to try and never make that mistake again.
- Have an older child share what he or she remembers about being baptized. The child could talk about preparing for baptism, what it feels like to be baptized, and what it means to become a member of the Church.

The temple: Temples help us become more like Heavenly Father. The scriptures tell us that the Lord's people have always built temples as sacred places for Jesus and Heavenly Father to visit on earth.

- I am preparing now to go to the temple someday.
- I know that temples are sacred places where families can be sealed together forever. That means that after we die, we will still be with our families. I want to live with my family forever.
- You could have an older child talk about family history research and how the child has learned to help look for and prepare names

for temple work. You could also invite a child who has attended a temple open house in the past to talk about the experience.

Song: "I Love to See the Temple"

My body is a temple: In 1 Corinthians, we learn that our bodies are temples for our spirits. We want to take good care of our bodies by staying physically healthy and spiritually clean. The scriptures teach us how to do these things.

- I can choose good music to listen to.
- I want to keep my body clean and my spirit pure. This means I need to be careful about the media I watch, read, and listen to. I know that the Holy Ghost can help me to know what media is good for me.
- Have an older child give a talk on the Word of Wisdom and how it has helped him or her to stay physically healthy. If appropriate, have the child draw the connection between physical addictions and other habits that can harm us spiritually. Ask the child to share his or her commitment to live virtuously.

Song: "The Lord Gave Me a Temple"

Missionary work: The scriptures tell us stories of great missionaries like Ammon and Paul. We are trying to become good missionaries by sharing the scriptures we love with the people we love and the new friends we meet.

- I want to serve a mission.
- I can be a missionary now by being a good example to my friends and family. I am preparing to serve a mission by studying the scriptures and getting ready to go to the temple someday. The gospel makes me happy, and I want others to be happy too!
- Ask an older child with a sibling who has served or is serving a mission to talk about his or her missionary sibling. Have the child discuss how his or her sibling prepared and how the family has been blessed by missionary service.

Prayer: When we pray, we know that Heavenly Father hears and answers us. Sometimes He gives us answers in the scriptures we read. We love to pray and talk to Heavenly Father every day.

- Heavenly Father hears me when I pray.
- I love to talk to Heavenly Father each day. I know that He answers my prayers. Sometimes my prayers are answered by other people, or in ways I'm not expecting.
- You might have an older child talk about a scripture story of someone who prayed and how that prayer was answered. Ask the child to include how this story helps his or her personal testimony that Heavenly Father always answers our prayers.

Song: "A Child's Prayer," or another song of your choice

Reverence: We can show reverence for sacred places and things by being quiet and still. We show reverence for the scriptures by taking good care of them and trying to do the things they say.

- Being reverent shows Heavenly Father I love Him.
- During the sacrament, I try to be reverent by thinking about Jesus. I know that He died for me, and I want to show Him by how I act that I honor and respect that sacrifice.
- You could have an older child talk about his or her personal commitment to keep the Sabbath day holy, including what kinds of activities can make the Sabbath a special day to feel the Spirit.

Jesus's birth and Second Coming: In the scriptures, we can read about Jesus's birth and Second Coming. We know that Jesus was born long ago as a baby. He grew up and learned, just like we do now. And we know that someday He will return to the earth, and we will all live in peace.

- I know Jesus will come again.
- Jesus came to live on the earth and set an example for us. Because Jesus was baptized, we know we all need to be baptized too. Jesus loved everyone, and I am trying to love everyone too.
- You might ask an older child to talk about what it means to live in the latter days. Have the child share his or her feelings about the Second Coming and the signs that will precede it. Make sure to emphasize that if we live righteously, we can look forward to the second coming with hope and excitement.

Song: "When He Comes Again," or another song of your choice

Closing remarks from a member of the bishopric.

About the Author

Heidi Doxey is the author of five volumes in the Tiny Talks series. Her debut novel, a young adult Jane Austen retelling, was released in May 2015. She is also the author of the board book *1, 2, 3 with Nephi and Me!*

Heidi lives in Utah, where she works as an editor, but she still thinks of the San Francisco Bay Area as home. She blogs at girlwithalltheanswers .blogspot.com.

You can also find Heidi online at PrimaryHelper.com, where she posts additional resources, ideas, and encouragement for Primary, FHE, and activities throughout the year.

SCAN to visit

WWW.PRIMARYHELPER.COM